JAPANESE

Learning the Origins of Beauty from
Hakone Museum of Art and Katsura Imperial Villa

GARDENS

SAKI KOSUGI · RYUICHI KOSUGI
FUMIHARU KOSUGI · ANDREAS HAMACHER

KOSUGI ZOHEN CO.LTD.

Bilingual Edition

日本庭園

箱根美術館、
桂離宮に学ぶ美の源流

日英対訳版

小杉左岐・小杉龍一
小杉文晴・ハマハ アンドレアス

著者　小杉造園株式会社

BANRAISHA

Prologue

In a Japanese garden, a miniaturized landscape of nature is presented in a reserved space, which we call 'niwa'. In this book, I will introduce two outstanding gardens so that people outside Japan will have the opportunity to see the beauty of Japanese gardens.

One is the garden of the Hakone Museum of Art. The garden, created by Mokichi Okada (founder of MOA), is one of the top-class gardens, blessed with the dynamic beauty of the surrounding nature of Hakone, and beauty created by human hands. The patio garden in Hakone's sister museum MOA Museum of Art is also worth visiting for its simplicity and refined design.

The other is the garden of Katsura Imperial Villa, formerly the country house of the Hachijo family. The garden startles guests with splendid construction techniques and the aesthetics of the tea ceremony ('wabi' and 'sabi'), all still so delicately preserved for almost 400 years.

Every year at Kosugi Zohen, we welcome students and professionals from abroad at our training facility in Atami, to offer Japanese garden seminar. I also go abroad to convey Japanese garden culture, technique and skills through lectures.

January 2017

Saki Kosugi
KOSUGI Kosugi Zohen Co., Ltd.
(http://www.kosugi-zohen.co.jp/)

The garden of Hakone Museum of Art harmonizes with mountains and Sagami Gulf (right)
箱根美術館は、箱根連山や相模灘（右側）の背景を一体とした庭である

はじめに

　日本の庭は、〝庭という限られた空間〟に、自然の風景を凝縮して取り入れてできた景観です。日本庭園の美しさを海外の皆さまに観ていただきたく、代表的な二つの庭をご紹介いたします。

　まず、箱根美術館の庭です。箱根美術館の庭は、MOAの創始者岡田茂吉が箱根の山水を生かした雄大かつ豪壮な自然美と、人の手による庭園美を融合させた日本では第一級の美しい庭です。姉妹館の熱海美術館の中庭にみられる光琳屋敷の質素で奥ゆかしい庭も推奨したい庭です。

　桂離宮の庭は八条宮家の別邸で、卓越した造園技術とわび・さびを感じさせる庭です。約400年前につくられた庭でありながら、今でも職人の手で行き届いた手入れがされており、美しいままに残っています。

　小杉造園では、毎年海外の多くの造園研修生を熱海の小杉造園研修センターに迎え、また諸外国から依頼され、日本の文化や造園の講演のために海外に出かけ、さまざまな文化と技術・技能を世界に伝えています。

　なお、本書の第1章、第3章の執筆にあたっては、MOA美術館の皆さまに大変お世話になりました。心より感謝申し上げます。

　2017年1月

　　　　　　　　　　　　　　　　KOSUGI　小杉造園株式会社　小杉左岐
　　　　　　　　　　　　　　　　　（http://www.kosugi-zohen.co.jp/）

The garden of Katsura Imperial Villa, created some 400 years ago, is highly renowned overseas
桂離宮の庭は約400年前につくられ、海外でも定評がある

Shirou M. Wakui
涌井史郎（雅之）

Landscape Architect
Distinguished Professor, Tokyo City University
President, Gifu Academy of Forest Science and Culture
Visiting Professor, Tokyo University of Agriculture

造園家・東京都市大学特別教授
岐阜県立森林文化アカデミー学長
東京農業大学客員教授

Foreward　賛歌

　"He who lights up a corner of a nation is the true treasure of a nation." The words of Dengyō Daishi (Saichō), the founder of Japanese Tendai Buddhism, perfectly describe Saki Kosugi, gardener and landscape architect. Born as a grandson of family of gardeners, Mr. Kosugi successfully expanded his family business. At the same time, perhaps driven by the enterprising spirit of quintessential Tokyo he inherited, Mr. Kosugi has been constructing Japanese gardens in foreign countries which are not major powers but have distinctive cultures and spiritual wealth. His activities abroad are not necessarily on a for-profit basis, so he is often referred to as a volunteer gardener diplomat. Mr. Kosugi loves Japanese gardening, one of the essences of Japanese culture, and he is an expert in the field. By creating a Japanese-style garden space, Mr. Kosugi wishes to spread the unique character of Japan's beauty, which values peace and treasures nature. It is like lighting a candle in the dark: The light of the candle illuminates the pure hearts of humanity, and brightens up the world. That is why he deserves to be called a treasure of a nation.

　「一隅を照らす之(これ)国宝」。庭師・造園家「小杉左岐」はまさにこの言葉そのものである。氏は三代目の家業造園業を発展させながら、江戸人の粋な遺伝子をも継ぎ、世界、それも大国というより独自の文化と心の豊かさを大切にしている国々に日本庭園を造り続けている。それは決して商売ではない。故に、ボランティアな造園外交官と称される。日本文化の粋である日本庭園を愛し、その技術を極めればこそ、彼が創造する庭園空間を通じ、平和で自然を慈しんでやまぬ日本美の特質を世界に伝播したいと、ただその義務感で造り続けている。まさに暗闇にろうそくの火を点じ、その明るさで人間の純なる心に灯をともし、世界を明るく彩ろうとしている。まさに国の宝といってよい。

Contents

Prologue　はじめに 2

Foreward　賛歌　涌井史郎 4

Chapter 1

Hakone Museum of Art
Strolling in the Shinsen-kyo
箱根美術館 ― 神仙郷を巡る

About　Shinsen-kyo garden　箱根美術館・神仙郷とは 10

Hakone Museum of Art　箱根美術館　10

Registered Monument of Japan　国の登録記念物　11

What to see in the garden　鑑賞のポイント 12

Marriage of natural and man-made beauty　自然美と人工美の融合　12

Suggested Route map　鑑賞のルート　13

Walking in the Shinsen-kyo　神仙郷を歩く 14

Moss-covered Valley in Mountain Recess　苔に覆われた深山の渓谷　14

Expansive sloped moss garden　苔庭の春夏秋冬　16

Enjoy moss garden view at Shinwa-tei　真和亭より苔庭を楽しむ　22

Design hints seen in Fujimi-tei　富士見亭に見る庭のデザイン　26

Classical pond garden beside Nikko-den　日光殿横の古典的な池泉庭　28

Kanzan-tei, Sekiraku-en rock garden　岩石の景を誇る観山亭と石楽園　30

Features in Kanzan-tei, Sangetsu-an　観山亭、山月庵の施設　34

Bamboo garden　雪竹図屏風をイメージさせる竹庭　36

Bush clover cottage, Bush clover path　初秋に見ごろの萩の家・萩の道　38

Sangetsu-an Tea House and Tea Garden　日本を代表する山月庵と茶庭　40

Shinzan-so, standing on a rock　岩の上に建つ神山荘　44

Visitor information　利用案内 45

Chapter 2
Katsura Imperial Villa
Strolling in the Garden
桂離宮 — 庭園を巡る

Katsura Imperial Villa　桂離宮の庭について　48
Katsura is a villa built by the Hachijo family　八条宮家による造営　48

Historical background　造営の歴史的背景　50

What to see in the garden　鑑賞のポイント　54
Miniaturized 'Ama no Hashidate'　天橋立の縮景　54
'Wabi' and 'Sabi'　「わび」と「さび」　55
Influence of Western culture in garden techniques　西洋文化の手法　56
Maintained over 400 years　400年間にわたる維持管理　57

Layout of the garden and key facilities　庭の配置図　58
Suggested Route map　鑑賞のルート　58
Fence of Katsura Imperial Villa　桂離宮の垣根　59

Stroll in the Garden　庭を巡る　60
Miyuki-mon, Miyuki-michi, Dobashi　御幸門、御幸道、土橋　60
Sumiyoshi Pine tree hiding the view of a pond　池泉の眺めを隠す住吉の松　62
Boating pond, boat hut (Ofunegoya)　舟遊びを楽しんだ池泉と御舟小屋　63
Momiji no baba, Soto Koshikake　紅葉の馬場、外腰掛　64
Cycas hill preparing for winter　蘇鉄山の冬支度　65
Stone beach, Pond as 'Ama no Hashidate'　洲浜と天橋立を模した池泉　66
Shokin-tei overlooking 'Ama no Hashidate'　天橋立を望む松琴亭　68
Shoka-tei looking down the pond　池泉を見下ろす賞花亭　70
Onrin-do (Mortuary tablet hall for the Hachijo family)　宮家の位牌を祀る園林堂　72
Shoi-ken, unique for its round windows　丸い窓が特徴の笑意軒　74
Shoin (Study halls) lined up like flying geese　雁行形に並ぶ書院群　76
Geppa-ro, the tea house for watching the moon　月を愛でる月波楼　78
'Chu-mon', Lindera umbellata fence　黒文字の垣根、中門　79
Okoshi yose (Main entrance of Study halls)　書院群の玄関、御輿寄　80

Visitor information　利用案内　81

Chapter 3

Three garden elements and ornamental items
of the Japanese garden
日本庭園 — 三要素と添景物

Pond: Core of the garden　庭の中心となる池泉 84
Japanese gardens evolved with pond　池泉を中心に発達した日本庭園　84
Garden waterfall　水の景を表わす庭滝　86
Garden bridges: A landscape accent　景観の視点になる庭橋　88

Stones: The Base of garden structure　庭の骨格をつくる石 90
Stones as dwellings of God　神が宿る場としての石　90
Placement of more than 2 stones　2つ以上の石を組み合わせる配石　91
Pavement, stairs, masonry of stone　草・行・真による敷石・石段・石積み　92
Stepping stones: How to ensure walkability　足元を確かにする飛石　94
Nobedan (stone-paved rectangular path)　足の運びを促し、足元を飾る延段　96

Plants add seasonal tastes　四季の風情を際立たせる植栽 98
Plant to form scalene triangles　不等辺三角形に植えて庭に動きを出す　98
Specimen tree　庭に生気を生み出す役木　100
Cold protection, support posts　草木を守る支柱と防寒　102

Ornamental items　庭の風景を引き締める添景物 104
Stone lanterns cast light on feet　足元を照らす石灯籠　104
Stone tower　庭に奥行きや広さを見せる石塔（層塔）　105
Fences, Sleeve fence　目隠しや仕切り直しに用いる庭垣や袖垣　106
'Tsukubai' and 'Chozubachi'　身を清める蹲踞と手水鉢　110
'Suikin-kutsu', 'Kakei', 'Shishi-odoshi'　音を楽しむ水琴窟・筧・鹿おどし　112

Tea room, Tea house　一期一会を楽しむ茶室・茶亭 114
Tea garden, Chatei and Chashitsu　茶庭・茶亭・茶室　114

Steps to enjoy light green tea　薄茶の飲み方 116

CHAPTER 1

HAKONE MUSEUM OF ART

Strolling in the Shinsen-kyo

箱根美術館 — 神仙郷を巡る

Kanzan-tei
観山亭

Shinsen-kyo garden is located on the grounds of the Hakone Museum of Art. Highly esteemed by professional gardeners as one of the first-class Japanese gardens, Shinsen-kyo is a joint work of Hakone's natural beauty formed by volcanic activity and the excellent skills of landscape gardeners under the direction of Mokichi Okada, founder of the Museum.

箱根美術館の苑内にある和風庭園・神仙郷は、
美術館の創立者である岡田茂吉の構想のもとに、
火山の噴火によって生まれた箱根の自然を生かした
日本では第一級の庭園です。
多くの庭師や造園家から高い評価を得ています。

About Shinsen-kyo garden 箱根美術館・神仙郷とは

Hakone Museum of Art 箱根美術館

Hakone Museum of Art was established in 1952 by Mokichi Okada in Gora, Hakone-town. Okada had a conviction that art works are not something exclusively possessed by individuals, but should be exhibited to as many people as possible, entertaining and enlightening visitors, and eventually contributing to the flourishing culture of Japan. Precious collections include earthenware of the Jomon period (15,000-1,000 BC), pots and jars of the Kamakura (1185-1333 CE) and Muromachi (1336 -1573 CE) periods at Six Old Kilns of Japan, and porcelains of the Edo (1603-1868 CE) period.

箱根美術館は、岡田茂吉が1952年、箱根町強羅に開館した美術館です。「美術品は決して独占すべきものではなく、一人でも多くの人に見せ、娯しませ、人間の品性を向上させる事こそ、文化の発展に大いに寄与する」という信念のもとに、縄文時代（紀元前15000〜前1000年）の土器や鎌倉（1185〜1333年）・室町時代（1336〜1573年）に制作された六古窯の壺や甕、江戸時代（1603〜1868年）の焼きものなど貴重な品々が展示され、公開されています。

Garden path in moss garden
苔庭の苑路

Registered Monument of Japan　国の登録記念物

　Okada purchased villa property from Raita Fujiyama, a notable businessman from Saga Prefecture, and the garden section of Gora Park in 1944, to develop Shinsen-kyo as a utopia, making the best use of the surrounding natural environment.　Shinsen-kyo was completed in 1953. In August 2013, Shinsen-kyo was designated as Registered Monument of Japan (scenic spot), as it is considered a landmark with excellent historical and cultural value.

　岡田茂吉は1944年に、佐賀出身の実業家・藤山雷太の別荘地や箱根・強羅公園の庭園部分を再整備し、箱根の自然環境の特質を生かした理想郷である神仙郷（1953年完成）を造営しました。この神仙郷は、歴史的、文化的価値が高い遺産として、2013年8月には、国の登録記念物（名勝地関係）に登録されています。

The garden is beautifully designed to incorporate with the natural environment of Hakone
庭園は箱根の自然環境を見事に取り入れている

What to see in the garden 鑑賞のポイント

Marriage of natural and man-made beauty 自然美と人工美の融合

On a 92,400-square-meter estate, Shinsen-kyo is made up of different types of gardens, and visitors can enjoy beautiful landscape as the seasons change:

Moss garden: Some 130 species of moss grow in an area where almost 200 maple (Japanese acer) trees are planted.

Bush Clover (Hagi, or *Lespedeza thunbergii*) Path leads to Bush Clover Cottage. Both sides of the Path are piles of rough natural stones and rocks, and Hagi shrubs hang over the stones.

Bamboo garden: A small space with lots of bamboo. The atmosphere has a touch of Chinese aesthetic.

Sekiraku-en: Surrounded by mountains and an expansive view of Sagami Gulf, the main feature of this area is stone arrangement. In November, when maple leaves in the moss garden turn breath-taking colors, Sekiraku-en, usually closed, is open on an extended schedule.

Among numerous great Japanese gardens, the unique character of Shinsen-kyo is a celestial integration of the Hakone area's magnificent natural beauty and outstanding works of gardeners which brought about a picturesque landscape, like the paintings of the Rinpa▼ school, a Japanese painting style that originated in the Momoyama period. The result is a garden which simultaneously soothes and entertains visitors.

9万2400㎡の敷地をもつ神仙郷には、約130種類の苔が生え、約200本のモミジが植えられている「苔庭」、野積みの岩をミヤギノハギが覆う「萩の道」と「萩の家」、中国風の庭園が広がる「竹庭」などがあり、四季折々の景観が楽しめます。モミジが素晴らしい11月には、四方に見える明神ヶ岳、明星ヶ岳、浅間山や相模灘を借景に、石組を中心に空間美を演出した「石楽園」も連日特別公開されています。

日本には多くの素晴らしい庭園がありますが、この神仙郷は単に見せるためだけの庭ではありません。箱根の雄大な山水の景観のよさを生かした自然美と、琳派の絵画▼の造園化ともいうべき造園の人工美が融合した、誰もが心を癒し楽しめる、親しみやすい世界を再現しているように思います。

▼ MOA Museum of Art in Atami holds a number of paintings from the Rimpa school, including "Red and White Plum Blossoms" folding screens painted by Korin Ogata.

▼熱海のMOA美術館には尾形光琳筆による国宝「紅白梅図屏風」など琳派の作品がある。

Suggested Route map 鑑賞のルート

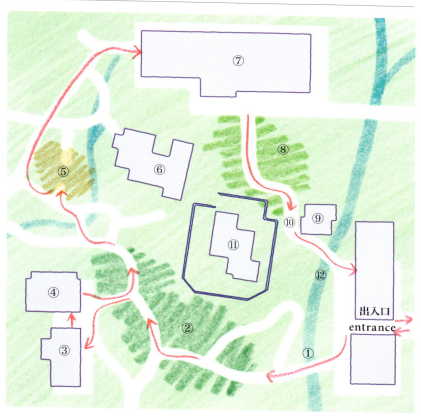

① Taiko-bashi (Arched bridge) ② Moss garden ③ Fujimi-tei (Mt. Fuji View Pavilion) ④ Shinwa-tei Tea House ⑤ Sekiraku-en Garden ⑥ Kanzan-tei (Mountain View Pavilion) ⑦ Main building of the Museum ⑧ Bamboo garden ⑨ Hagino-ya (Bush Clover Cottage) ⑩ Bush Clover Path ⑪ Sangetsu-an Tea House ⑫ Yatsu-hashi

① 太鼓橋 ② 苔庭 ③ 富士見亭 ④ 茶室・真和亭 ⑤ 石楽園 ⑥ 観山亭 ⑦ 本館
⑧ 竹庭 ⑨ 萩の家 ⑩ 萩の道 ⑪ 茶室・山月庵 ⑫ 八橋

* On the map, two facilities (Nikko-den and Shinzan-so) are not shown, as they are usually not open to the visitors.

* 真和亭・富士見亭の裏には日光殿、石楽園の奥には神山荘がありますが、通常は非公開なので、地図上では省きます。

Chapter 1 Hakone Museum of Art / 箱根美術館   13

Walking in the Shinsen-kyo 神仙郷を歩く

Moss-covered Valley in Mountain Recess 苔に覆われた深山の渓谷

Passing through the main gate and to the left along the stone-paved path, visitors may feel as if they are lost deep in the mountains. As they stand over the gently-arched bridge and look into the valley under their feet, they will see rapids and rocks, large and small, arranged to form banks. Hakone has primarily been blessed with a natural landscape and diverse species of plants.

Okada had a clear intention "to break the old rules of gardening and establish a new style, free from rigid framework." To create a landscape by making the most use of Hakone's environment, a dynamic art in itself, Okada built the garden so that visitors will understand their own inherent viewpoints about beauty.

表門から石貼り(石畳)の道を左に進むとすぐに、深山に迷い込んだような錯覚を覚えます。反りが優しく女性的な太鼓橋に立てば、苑内を突っ切る渓流と荒々しい大小の奇岩が護岸石組を成して、眼前に迫ってきます。箱根はもともと自然の景観に優れ、多種多様な植物に恵まれているところで、作庭の意図は、「昔からの庭造りの約束を破り、型にとらわれない新しい形式」でした。人の手を加えなくても雄大な芸術でもある自然を生かして景観をつくりあげ、「見る人が自分に内在している美の観点を引き出し」ていくことを狙いとしています。

Deep valley and rough stones
渓谷と荒々しい岩

Stone-paved garden path leads to arched bridge
石貼りの道に続く太鼓橋

Above: View over arched bridge from valley
上：渓谷から太鼓橋を見る

Below: Moss-covered rocks
下：苔むした奇岩の数々

 In constructing the Shinsen-kyo garden, Okada was quoted as saying that he carefully chose combinations of stones, species of trees and grasses, and placed all of them carefully as if he "were drawing a painting using natural materials." Human touches in a rough great nature provide contrast to those who visit the garden.

 「巌の組み合わせ、樹木や草なども選びに選び抜いて、一々に心を籠めてあしらい、恰も自然の材料で絵を描くよう」に作庭したといわれます。自然の荒々しさの中に心を込めた人の手が入り、それによりにじみ出る優しさが感じられ、どの方向から見ても心が癒されます。

Chapter 1 Hakone Museum of Art / 箱根美術館

Expansive sloped moss garden 苔庭の春夏秋冬

On the right side of stone-paved garden path lies a gentle but spacious slope, covered with some 130 types of beautiful green moss. The sky above the slope is overcast by almost 200 towering maple trees, as if competing with moss. Many gardeners praise the scenery as "threedimentional beauty, like a raised painting of Korin Ogata, a renowned painter in the Edo period." As visitors walk through the tunnel of maple trees and moss, another world of clear blue sky and green moss-covered earth emerges, leading the way to Shinwa-tei.

　石貼りの苑道の右手には緩やかなスロープになった広大な苔庭が広がります。地表には約130種類の青々とした苔が生え、約200本のモミジの高木が天を覆うように植えられています。まさに苔とモミジの饗宴です。「尾形光琳の絵をたち上げたような立体的な美の庭園」と、多くの作庭家や庭師が称賛する風景です。苔庭とモミジのトンネルを抜けると、ぱっと広がるのは青い空と明るい緑の苔の大地、真和亭などにつながる別世界です。

Spring

Rolling hills clad in verdure of moss and
tall maple trees clothed in fresh green leaves fill
the cheerful and airy time
in the garden.

起伏に富んだ青々とした苔の大地と
新緑をまとったモミジの高木が
明るく軽やかな時を満たしてくれる。

初夏

Early summer

Illusionary scene of the moss garden.
A huge rock placed in the moss garden,
sitting gently with hints of inner strength,
indicates momentum.

幻想的な苔庭。
苔庭に据えられた大岩が、優しさの中にも力強さを秘め、
勢いの「気」を感じる。

秋
Autumn

Autumnal tints of maple leaves show brilliant contrasts with the green color of moss. To take away fallen maple leaves scattered over the moss, they do not use brooms but hand-pick them: a tiny warmth of handiwork.

苔の緑と鮮やかなコントラストを見せるモミジが美しい。
苔の上に落ちるモミジの枯葉は手でかき集め、
ほうきを使わないといわれる。手のぬくもりが生きている。

Chapter 1 Hakone Museum of Art / 箱根美術館　　19

冬
Winter

Snow drifts over the moss garden.
The view reminds us of a quiet yet touching
drawing by Buson Yosa, one of eminent
Japanese artists during the Edo period.

雪に覆われた苔庭。
与謝蕪村が描いたような、
心に迫る一幅の絵画を思わせる。

Enjoy moss garden view at Shinwa-tei 真和亭より苔庭を楽しむ

From Shinwa-tei tea house, visitors will enjoy a full view of the moss garden they just strolled through. Not a single fleck of dust can be found in the garden, the visitors will be impressed how well-kept the garden is.

真和亭の茶室では、散策してきた苔庭を一望することができます。庭には塵一つ
なく、また、手入れの行き届いた草や樹木に庭園管理の素晴らしさを感じます。

The earth in the garden is overlayed with moss and stone pavement,
a beautiful combination and contrast of nature and human skill
大地を苔や石畳でカバーし、自然と人工の対比が美しい

Shinwa-tei seen from moss garden
苔庭から見る真和亭

Placement of moss around tree base
苔による樹木の根締め

Stepping stones of different materials
異なる飛石材

Chapter 1 Hakone Museum of Art / 箱根美術館

As visitors follow stepping stones in the Shinwa-tei tea house, they will reach a rustic tea room. A simple bamboo-slit door and 'Yotsume-gaki' (four-eyed fence) divide outer and inner tea gardens, and a waiting shelter is set in the inner garden. Guests will get prepared here for the tea ceremony, and await the host's call. Please pay attention to the placement of stepping stones at the shelter. Distance between stones affects walking speed, and guides people's movement. In setting stepping stones, Sen no Rikyu, Japan's tea master who perfected tea ceremony culture, is said to have put more emphasis on walkability than on appearance, 6 to 4, while Oribe Furuta, Japan's warrior and tea ceremony master in the Edo period, is believed to have held higher account for appearance than for walkability, 6 to 4.

真和亭の飛石を辿ると、ひなびた茶室に行きつきます。外露地と内露地の間には簡素な枝折戸(木戸)と四ツ目垣があり、内露地には腰掛が設けられています。客人はここでお茶をいただく準備をし、主人の案内を待ちます。

腰掛下の飛石の据え方に注意しましょう。飛石は歩く速さを決め、人の動きをコントロールします。茶の湯を広めた千利休は「わたり(歩きやすさ)六分、景(美観)四分」といって実用を重んじ、茶を極めた古田織部は「わたり四分、景六分」として美観を重んじたとされます。

Guests follow stepping stones to reach the tea room. A bamboo-slit door and 'Yotsume-gaki' (four-eyed fence) separate outer and inner tea gardens
客人は茶室に入るために飛石を歩く。内露地との間には枝折戸と四ツ目垣がある

Guests walk down stepping stones again in the inner garden. In the waiting shelter, they prepare to attend the tea ceremony, and await the host's call. Stepping stones at the shelter are placed to not disturb other guests

内露地に入り、飛石を再び歩み、腰掛で茶をいただく準備をし、主人の案内を待つ。飛石は他の客人に迷惑をかけないように据えられている

Guests walk down 'nobedan' (stone pavement), place their shoes on the shoe-removing stone, and enter the tea room through crawl-in entrance with heads lowered, showing respects to the host

客人は延段を歩み、沓脱石で履物を脱ぎ、躙(にじ)り口より頭を下げて入り、主人に礼儀を尽くす

Design hints seen in Fujimi-tei 富士見亭に見る庭のデザイン

Fujimi-tei is the former Tokyo residence of Mokichi Okada, founder of the garden, brought over to Hakone. Facilities and ornamental items placed in Fujimi-tei garden show a lot of examples of garden design: "Teppo-gaki" (bamboo musket fence), which connects Shinwa-tei and Fujimi-tei, an open gutter to soften mud splashing and cobbles in the gutter to moderate rain drop sounds, "Koetsuji gaki" (open woven bamboo fence) used as a separation, standing hand wash basin placed under eaves, stone stairs made of natural stones and paved with pebbles as exposed-aggregate finish to call for attention at the foot.

　富士見亭は、創立者・岡田茂吉が昭和11(1936)年から9年間過ごした東京・上野毛の執務室を移築したものです。一般住居に見られる庭のしつらいに、参考になるところがたくさんあります。例えば、隣り合う真和亭と富士見亭を取り持つ鉄砲垣、雨だれの泥はねを緩和する明渠に小石を置いて雨音を鎮める心配り、区切りに用いる光悦寺垣、軒下に設けられた手を清めるための立ち手水鉢、石段に用いた自然石と砂利の洗い出しを使った足元への注意喚起など、和の庭に見られるさまざまな添景物や設備が施されています。

Fujimi-tei with "Koetsuji-gaki" bamboo fence
富士見亭と光悦寺垣

"Teppo-gaki" between Shinwa-tei, Fujimi-tei
真和亭と富士見亭を結ぶ鉄砲垣

Standing hand wash basin
立ち手水鉢

Open gutter to soften rain drop sounds
雨落ちを配慮する明渠

Natural stone stair and cobblestone pavement
自然石の石段と砂利の洗い出し（霰こぼし）による石貼り

Chapter 1 Hakone Museum of Art / 箱根美術館

Classical pond garden beside Nikko-den 日光殿横の古典的な池泉庭

 Nikko-den is a facility for classical theater performances and other events, designed by Isoya Yoshida, a renowned Japanese architect. A classical pond garden beside Nikko-den is a must to visit. The style is called "Tsuru Kame Horai" (Crane, tortoise, and Mt. Penglai). The crane and tortoise are symbols of longevity, and Mt. Penglai is a sacred mountain in old Chinese legend, believed to be a place of eternal youth and immortality. In the garden, "Horai" stone, said to be the largest piece in Shinsen-kyo, is placed beside the large pond, and the crane stone and tortoise stone are sitting on both sides. Behind the arrangement, a waterfall named "Ryuzu" pours a streak of water into the pond. This stone arrangement style illustrates a great deal of auspiciousness, like a mirage which man would never be able to possess.

 日光殿は建築家の吉田五十八の設計によるもので、古典芸能などを楽しむ場所です。この日光殿の横にある池泉庭は見逃してはならない庭の一つで、鶴亀蓬莱の庭といいます。大きな池には、苑内で最も巨大といわれる蓬莱石と鶴石と亀石が配されています。その奥には龍頭の滝があり、一条の遣り水が池泉に注ぎます。これは蓬莱の立石を中心に鶴亀石で構成される石組で、大いなるめでたさを表現しています。人間が求めても求め得られない蜃気楼のようなめでたさということです。

'Horai-seki' (largest piece on right-end), 'Kame-ishi'(below 'Horai-seki'), 'Tsuru-ishi' (left-end)
右端の大きな石が蓬莱石、その下が亀石、左端が鶴石

Above: Nikko-den
上：日光殿

Below left: Dragon's head waterfall at the bottom of pond
下左：奥に見えるのが龍頭の滝

Below right: Floating water lily
下右：水面（みずも）に浮かぶスイレン

Chapter 1 Hakone Museum of Art / 箱根美術館   29

Kanzan-tei, Sekiraku-en rock garden   岩石の景を誇る観山亭と石楽園

Hakone area has long been a land of lava strata, created by the eruptions of Mt. Soun. The maple tree and moss garden, now on a gentle slope, used to be covered with jagged rocks of all sizes. The founders of the garden removed such rocks one by one and piled up soil, to produce the present landscape.

In contrast to the creation process of the maple and moss garden, Sekiraku-en, the stone garden, shows the old landscape of the area by keeping the original conditions. Kanzan-tei stands in the heart of Sekiraku-en, a traditional residence built in sukiyazukuri style ("sukiya" means tea house). The design of Kanzan-tei was partly created by Isoya Yoshida, one of Japan's renowned architects. The name "Kanzan" came from the splendid location where visitors can enjoy panoramic views of Hakone mountains such as Mt. Soun and Mt. Myojin, as well as the Sagami Gulf.

もともと箱根一帯は、早雲山の噴火による岩石が累々と堆積した土地でした。今まで紹介した苔庭とモミジの林も、今はなだらかなスロープですが、かつては大小のごつごつした岩が転がっており、それらを一つ一つ取り除いて盛り土して今の景観をつくりだしたといわれます。そうした岩場を今に残して、岩の庭として作庭されているのが、神仙郷の奥庭といわれる石楽園です。その中心にあるのが吉田五十八設計（一部）による数寄屋建築の観山亭。早雲山や明神岳などの箱根の山々や相模灘まで見渡すことができることから、この名があります。

Clounds hanging low over Hakone mountains and Sagami Gulf, seen from Kanzan-tei
観山亭から見る箱根の山々と相模灘（中央）に雲がかかる

Looking up Kanzan-tei from stone stair bottom
飛石状の階段の先に見える観山亭

Kanzan-tei
観山亭

Entrance to front garden of Kanzan-tei
観山亭の前庭入口

Chapter 1 Hakone Museum of Art / 箱根美術館

Hakone somma as borrowed scenery
箱根の外輪山を借景に

Huge stones sit along the garden path
巨石が横たわる苑路

Stone and plant arrangement
石組と植栽

Stone bridge set beside gigantic stones
巨石の脇の石橋

Water stream falling between rocks
岩の間を流れ落ちる遣水（やりみず）

On both sides of the stepping-stone path, which leads to the Kanzan-tei, visitors will find unbelievably huge rocks and moss-covered stones. A mountain stream runs nearby, and the space between the path and the stream is filled with myriad trees and flowers, an extraordinary landscape not commonly seen.

The amazing feature of this area is that the border between man-made garden and genuine nature is rather hard to define, and visitors will not easily get bored. So impressed by the integration of nature and man-made beauty, visitors will, unconsciously, contemplate the intention of garden design.

観山亭への飛石状の苑路を、まさかと思われるような大きな奇岩や苔むした岩が横たわって挟み撃ちにしています。近くを渓流が流れ、その間を樹木や草花が埋め尽くし、今まで見たこともない天地が広がります。どこまでが庭でどこからが自然なのか、見当もつきにくく、視線を飽きさせない作庭には目を見張ります。自然と人工美の融合に大きな感動を覚えながら、誰もがこれが作庭の意図かと改めて考えさせられるのではないでしょうか。

'Sukiya-zukuri'

'Sukiya-zukuri'('Sukiya' style) is a style of Japanese architecture originating in the Muromachi period and early Edo period (1336-1691), when tea ceremony culture grew popular ('sukiya' means tea house). In Sukiya style, a tea house is incorporated into a Samurai residence. Sukiya style is known for its simple, elegant appearance, generally reflecting the tastes of the owner.

〈数寄屋造り〉

数寄屋造りは、室町時代から江戸時代初期(1336〜1691年)、茶の湯の流行に伴い、武家屋敷に茶室を取り入れた建築様式です。好みにまかせて造った、簡素で風流なたたずまいが特徴です。

Chapter 1 Hakone Museum of Art / 箱根美術館

Features in Kanzan-tei, Sangetsu-an 観山亭、山月庵の施設

At Kanzan-tei, built under modern sukiya-zukuri style, and Sangetsu-an, which houses a tea room, some ornamental items are so attractive that they may fit to modern living style: sodegaki (sleeve fence), lighting lantern, and waiting shelter. Let us introduce some examples which are suitable for architectures of both Japanese and western styles.

現代的な数寄屋造りを取り入れた観山亭と茶室のある山月庵では、袖垣、灯り灯籠、腰掛など私たちの生活に取り入れても面白いと思えるものがたくさんあります。和風建築ばかりでなく洋風建築にも取り入れてみるなど、エキゾチックな趣も楽しめる、気持ちが落ち着ける庭の設備を紹介します。

Above left: Sleeve fence using black bamboo stalks
上左：黒穂垣の袖垣

Above right: Sleeve fence made with yotsumegaki bamboo fence
上右：四つ目垣の袖垣

Below: Shiori-do (wicket) made with yaraigaki bamboo fence and yotsumegaki
下：矢来垣の枝折戸と四つ目垣

Sodegaki   Sodegaki (sleeve fence) is used for purposes similar to those of a lattice. By using natural materials such as bamboo stalks and paying attention to the balance with the architecture, you can make a garden with a unique taste.

袖垣　袖垣はラティスと同じような使い方をします。竹穂など自然のものを使用し、建造物などとバランスを取ると、一味違った庭造りができます。

Lighting lantern
灯り灯籠

Lighting lantern A lighting lantern is a stone lantern placed at corners and other points along the garden path for lighting at night. Trees and other greens are planted behind for a decorative arrangement.

灯り灯籠 灯り灯籠は夜間の明り取りのための灯籠です。曲がり角など苑路の要所において道案内をします。昼間は背後に木などを添えて庭の飾りとします。

Guests wait to be called in the shelter
客人は腰掛で呼び出しを待つ

Waiting shelter
腰掛

Waiting shelter A waiting shelter is built in inner and outer tea gardens, where tea ceremony guests prepare and wait for the host to call. If built without walls, a waiting shelter can be used as rustic thatched hut.

腰掛 腰掛は茶庭の外露地や内露地に置いてあり、ここで身支度をしたり、亭主の案内を待ったりします。また、茶庭でなくても吹きさらしの場所に設置して、四阿（あずまや）として使うこともできます。

Bamboo garden in winter　冬の竹庭

Bamboo garden　雪竹図屏風をイメージさせる竹庭

Leaving the main building of the Museum and walking down the garden path to the left, visitors will find bamboo gardens on both sides. A huge piece of rock, blanketed with moss, shows a beautiful contrast with a white gravel surface, and lots of fresh-green bamboo covers the whole garden. If seen in black and white, it would remind us of Chinese-style landscape painting. The design also reminds visitors of paintings including "Snow and Bamboo" by Korin Ogata, a notable painter in the Edo period.

　本館を背に、左手に進むと苑路の両側に竹庭が見えてきます。苔むす巨大な岩が露面だけを見せて白玉石敷と対比を成し、青々とした孟宗竹が庭全体を覆う、これがモノクロなら山水画に見るような竹庭です。尾形光琳の雪竹図屏風などをイメージさせる庭です。

Above: Bamboo garden paved by round cobbles
上：玉石が敷き詰められた竹庭

Below: Simple beauty of rock and bamboo
下：岩と竹の簡素な美しさ

Bush clover cottage, Bush clover path　初秋に見ごろの萩の家・萩の道

Once visitors pass through the bright green bamboo garden, they will be greeted with the Japanese bush clover path. In mid-September, bush clover reaches its full bloom, hanging over large stones piled up on both sides of the garden path. Bush clover cottage, a rent cottage constructed in neighboring Gora Park during the Taisho period (1912-1926) and later relocated here, stands along the garden path.

明るい緑の竹庭を抜けると、広がる光景は、萩の道です。初秋には、階段状の苑路に沿って配される野積みの巨大な石におおいかぶさるようにミヤギノハギが咲きます。その脇には、大正時代（1912〜1926年）に強羅公園にあった貸別荘を移築した萩の家もあります。ハギは9月中旬が見頃です。

Bush clover blooming over piled rocks
野積みの石にハギがおおいかぶさる萩の道

Fine display of bush clover
咲き乱れるハギ

Bush clover cottage
萩の家

Sangetsu-an Tea House and Tea Garden   日本を代表する山月庵と茶庭

Sangetsu-an is a tea house, built by illustrious tea house contractor Seibei Kimura Ⅲ, who was an expert in tea house design and construction.

Sangetsu-an was intended to spread Japan's tea ceremony culture globally, and has a thatched square roof, a small 3-tatami mat room, an 8-mat room and a garden.

山月庵は、茶の湯を国際的に普及させる目的で、茶室造りの名匠といわれる三代目・木村清兵衛によって造られた日本を代表する茅葺方形造りの茶室です。草庵風三畳の小間、書院風八畳の広間、庭園から構成されています。

Stone pathway to Sangetsu-an   山月庵の延段

Tea house at Sangetsu-an
山月庵の茶室

Stone pathway of Sangetsu-an and
trees planted at fence-end for accent
山月庵の敷石と垣留めの木

Mid-gate of Sangetsu-an
山月庵の中門

Stepping stones
and hand wash basin
飛石と蹲踞

Waiting shelter
with divided seats
割り腰掛

Chu-mon
中門

Tea house at Sangetsu-an
山月庵の茶室

   The tea garden of Sangetsu-an is double-type, which has both inner and outer gardens. In the inner garden, the waiting shelter has divided seats, one for notable guests and the other for the attendants. Stepping stones surrounding the hand wash basin are placed in a unique design.

   Yakuboku, or trees which are given different functions respectively, are deliberately planted: trees placed near the tea house, trees planted close to the window of the stone lantern, and trees planted around the hand wash basin, for example.

   茶庭は伝統的な外露地と内露地の二重露地になっており、内露地には身分の高い人用の貴人席と、そのお伴の相伴席がある割り腰掛があります。また、心身を清める蹲踞をめぐる飛石は巴にうねり、独特な意匠になっています。庵の近くに植える庵添えの木、石灯籠の火口に掛かるように植える灯障りの木、蹲踞や手水鉢に添えるように植える鉢囲いの木など、役木の取り決めなどもきちんと守られています。

Chapter 1 Hakone Museum of Art / 箱根美術館　　43

Shinzan-so, standing on a rock   岩の上に建つ神山荘

Shinzan-so is a relocated villa built by industrialist Raita Fujiyama in the early Taisho period (1912-1926). The house consists of three thatched-roof buildings. The whole house stands on a huge piece of rock, overlooking the whole Shinsen-kyo garden. Shinzan-so was registered as national tangible cultural property in 2001.

神山荘は、実業家・藤山雷太が大正初期（1910年代）に建てた別荘建築で、三棟の草葺き屋根から構成されています。家自体が大きな岩の上に立ち、苑内の景観を眺めることができます。2001年国の登録有形文化財に指定されました。

Shinzan-so 神山荘

Thatched roofs of three buildings
三棟の茅葺き屋根

Stairs made of natural stones
自然石を組み込んだ階段

Visitor information 利用案内

Web site　ホームページ
http://www.moaart.or.jp/

Location　場所
250-0408 1300 Gora, Hakone-machi, Ashigara Shimo-gun, Kanagawa Pref.
Tel. 0460-82-2623

〒250-0408　神奈川県足柄下郡箱根町強羅1300
電話　0460-82-2623

Transportation　交通
[From Shinjuku] Take Odakyu Line (Limited Express Romancecar) and get off at Odawara station. Or take Shinkansen bullet train from Tokyo or Shinagawa, and get off at Odawara station. Transfer to Hakone Tozan Train and go to Gora, change again to Cable car at Gora and get off at Koen-kami station. 1 minute walk from station.

［新宿から］小田急ロマンスカーで小田原下車。または東京もしくは品川から東海道新幹線で小田原下車。小田原からは箱根登山線で小田原〜強羅、ケーブルカーで強羅〜公園上駅下車、徒歩1分。

Opening hours　開館時期
Apr. to Nov. 9:30 〜 16:30 (admission until 16:00)
Dec. to Mar. 9:30 〜 16:00 (admission until 15:30)
Closed on Thu. (if Thu is national holiday, it is open), year-end and New Year.

開館　4月〜11月　9:30〜16:30（入場は16:00まで）
　　　12月〜3月　9:30〜16:00（入場は15:30まで）
休館　木曜日（木曜日が祝日の場合は開館）、年末年始

※Hakone Museum of Art has a 'sister' museum in the City of Atami, Shizuoka Prefecture.
※静岡県熱海市にも姉妹館があります。

CHAPTER 2

KATSURA IMPERIAL VILLA

Strolling in the Garden

桂離宮 — 庭園を巡る

View of Shoin(study halls), Geppa-ro from pond
池泉から見る書院群や月波楼

Katsura Imperial Villa was established as a country villa of the Imperial Hachijo family, approximately 400 years ago. Its garden was built during the Azuchi Momoyama period through early phase of the Edo period (toward the end of the 16th century to early 17th century). Even centuries after the initial opening, the deliberately planned garden design and excellent techniques used in construction to realize the design concept still earn high praise from landscape professionals as well as visitors.

桂離宮はおよそ400年前に造営された八条宮家の
別荘(当時は別業などと呼ばれた)です。この庭園は安土桃山時代から
江戸時代初期(16世紀末〜17世紀初期)に作庭されました。
考え抜かれた庭園デザインとそれを実現する造園技術の高さは、
今でも評判を呼んでいます。

Katsura Imperial Villa 桂離宮の庭について

Katsura is a villa built by the Hachijo family 八条宮家による造営

　Construction first started in 1615 by Prince Toshihito of the Hachijo family, in a Kyoto suburb named "Katsura", on the right bank of Katsura River. The Villa was repaired and expanded, starting in around 1641, by Prince Toshitada, son of Prince Toshihito. The Villa and its garden were planned to invite ex-Emperor Go-Mizunoo, the 108th Emperor during the Edo period and nephew of Toshihito. Ex-Emperor Go-Mizunoo visited Katsura Imperial Villa after Prince Toshihito passed away, and started to construct his own villa, Shugakuin Imperial Villa. Shugakuin has a reputation as the culmination of dynasty culture.

　桂離宮は京都市の郊外、桂川西岸の「桂」の地に、1615年ごろ、天皇の一族である八条宮智仁親王により着手され、さらに智仁親王の長男である智忠親王によって修復と造営が行われました。造営の目的は、江戸時代の第108代天皇で、智仁親王の甥にあたる後水尾上皇を招くための庭づくりといわれます。後水尾上皇は、智仁親王が崩御された後に正式に桂離宮を訪れ、その後、自ら王朝文化の極致といわれる雄大な修学院離宮を造営しています。

Pond surrounded by garden features such as bank and stone arrangement
護岸や石組など技巧に富む池泉風景

Stone arrangement symbolyzing 'Ariso' (seashore)
荒磯(ありそ)を表す石組

View of pond with bridge and island
橋や島の見える池泉の風景

Chapter 2 Katsura Imperial Villa / 桂離宮   49

Historical background 造営の歴史的背景

Katsura, a key junction of land and water transport
桂はかつて水・陸の交通の要所

Katsura, a key junction of land and water transport Katsura Imperial Villa is located in a western suburb of Kyoto, called 'Shimo Katsura' village at the time of construction. The area was on the west bank of Katsura River, one of the major rivers running through Kyoto. There was a small ferry on the east side to carry travelers and visitors. Upstream from the ferry, there was a distribution center of lumbers produced in Tanba, further upstream. A major road, Tanba-kaido Road connecting Kyoto and western part of Japan, ran along the south side of Katsura Imperial Villa. Katsura River merges into Yodo River in the south, leading to Amagasaki. Thus, Katsura Imperial Villa was built at a key junction of land and water transport. The Hachijo family was the owner of the Katsura area, and part of the profits earned at the ferry and lumber distribution center is believed to have financially supported the family.

桂離宮がある、当時「下桂村」と呼ばれていた地域は、都を流れる大きな川の一つ、桂川の西岸にあります。東岸には「桂の渡し」があり、そのすぐ上は「桂筏浜」と呼ばれる丹波から京都へ運ばれる木材の集積地でした。桂離宮の南側には山陰と京都を結ぶ丹波街道が通り、また桂川を南に下ればやがて淀川から尼崎にも通じ、まさに水・陸の交通の要所です。八条宮家はこの地を領有しており、「桂の渡し」や「桂筏浜」からの一部収益は宮家を支えていたといわれます。

Notable site of moon watching, illustrated in "The Tale of Genji"
『源氏物語』の桂殿の舞台となった月の名所

West bank of the Katsura River has long been known as a notable site for moon watching. Japanese tend to find something spiritual about the Moon, so many poems have been written about the Moon for centuries. By the Heian period (794-1192), many villas had been built by the aristocracy around Katsura area, solely for the purpose of enjoying the best view for moon watching.

Even Michinaga Fujiwara, one of the most powerful aristocrats in the Heian period who is believed to have patronized Murasaki Shikibu, author of "The Tale of Genji", and Sei Shonagon, a prominent female poet, had his own villa in Katsura. In Chapter 'Matsukaze' of the Tale of Genji, hero 'Hikaru Genji' has a country house 'Katsura-dono', which is said to have been modeled after the villa of Michinaga Fujiwara.

Centuries later, Prince Toshihito of Hachijo family, who is talented with poetry, built his own villa in Katsura, a spot ancient peerages admired so passionately. In the Villa, Prince Toshihito built a moon viewing terrace in the Old Study Hall, and other locations around the pond, 'Geppa-ro', 'Shokin-tei' and 'Shoi-ken', were also suitable for moon viewing.

桂川の西岸は、昔から月の名所でした。月に特別な精神性を見出す日本では、月にたくして多くの詩歌が詠まれています。同時に、平安時代にはすでに貴族の別荘が点在し、例えば左大臣として政権を掌握するだけでなく、文人であり紫式部や清少納言を庇護したとされる藤原道長の別荘「桂家」もありました。日本の古典、紫式部の『源氏物語』の「松風」の中に見られる光源氏の別荘「桂殿」は、桂家がお手本といわれます。

それから数百年がたち、詩歌に長じた八条宮智仁親王は、この月の名所、桂の地に別荘を造営しました。桂離宮の古書院には月見台が設けられ、古書院の北の月波楼、池の東の松琴亭、南の笑意軒からも、桂の月を楽しむことができました。

Moon viewing veranda
月見台

Life of Prince Toshihito, tossed about by fate
八条宮智仁親王の不幸

Despite so many high expectations for his future, Prince Toshihito never stood out in history, because of two misfortunes.

Prince Toshihito was born as the sixth child of the first crown prince of the Emperor, during the era of Shogun Hideyoshi Toyotomi. At the age of around 9, father of Prince Toshihito passed away and his brother inherited the throne (Emperor Go-Yozei). Shogun Hideyoshi Toyotomi, having no children, decided to adopt Prince Toshihito, only to change his mind a year later when his wife got pregnant.

Almost ten years after, Emperor Go-Yozei was planning to abdicate the throne to his younger brother Toshihito. Shogun Ieyasu Tokugawa strongly opposed to the idea, partly because next Emperor was already chosen by his government (Prince Katahito, first son of Emperor Go-Yozei).

Thus, Prince Toshihito was forced to pull himself down from the forefront of history.

桂離宮の造営者、智仁親王は、ふたつの不幸な出来事により、将来を期待されながらも表舞台に立つことがなく、時代に翻弄された人物といわれます。

親王が天皇の第一皇子の第六子として生まれたのは、豊臣秀吉が天下を治めたころのことです。

一つは親王が8歳から10歳のころのこと。即位することになっていた父が病死し、代わりに兄が後陽成天皇となったこともあり、親王は子どもに恵まれない秀吉の養子になります。将来は関白の職を期待されていました。しかし、その後秀吉に子どもが生まれたことから計画は破棄され、養子縁組は解消されてしまいます。

もう一つは18歳のころのことです。兄の後陽成天皇が退位するに当たり、天皇である兄の希望で次の天皇は弟の智仁親王に譲るという話が出ます。しかし、次の天皇は兄の長子の良仁親王と決まっていたこともあり、内大臣であった徳川家康らの強い反対もあって実現しませんでした。

こうして、智仁親王はやむなく歴史の舞台から降りることになります。

Revived 'garden salon' seen in dynastic culture
王朝文化の庭園サロンを再現

Prince Toshihito, being under the tutelage of Yusai Hosokawa, one of the best poets of the age, on "Kokin Wakashu" (anthology of short Japanese poem) and "The Tale of Genji", was blessed with outstanding talent for poetry and music, as well as having profound insight in architecture and gardening. Suden Ishin, prominent monk of Nanzen-ji Temple, illustrated a scene he witnessed upon his visit to the Katsura Imperial Villa, where boats were floating in the pond filled with water taken from Katsura River, like the boating pond gardens built during the dynasty age for poem reading and music.

During the era of Prince Toshitada (son of Toshihito), it was illustrated in "Kakumei-ki", a diary written by Rokuonji Temple (Kinkakuji, Temple of the Golden Pavilion) priest Shosho Horin, whom Toshitada himself served tea for guests, had drinks at five tea houses in the garden, and enjoyed boating in the pond.

智仁親王は、当代一流の歌人といわれた細川幽斎から『古今和歌集』や『源氏物語』の講義を受け、小さいころより詩歌に優れた才能を発揮し、また建築や造園にも造詣が深い文人でした。桂離宮を訪れた南禅寺の以心崇伝は、桂川の水を引いた桂離宮の池に（王朝時代の舟遊式庭園のように詩歌管弦を楽しみながら庭をめぐるための）船が浮かんでいるという情景を記しています。

次いで桂離宮を修理・造営した智仁親王の長男、智忠親王の時代、鹿苑寺（金閣寺）の鳳林承章が記した日記『隔蓂記』には、智忠親王自らお点前で茶をふるまい、庭に点在する5箇所のお茶屋で酒を飲み、舟で遊興を楽しんだというくだりがあります。

What to see in the garden　鑑賞のポイント

Miniaturized 'Ama no Hashidate'　天橋立の縮景

Under the Villa construction plan, a pond was first excavated on the 70,000-square-meter premises for boating, filled with water taken in from Katsura River. They built 'hills' and 'valleys' with excavated soil to form undulations in the garden.

On the east side of the pond, in front of the Shokin-tei tea house, a small landscape of 'Ama no Hashidate' ("Bridge of Heaven", one of the three most famous scenic places in Japan) was designed with stone bridges and splendid stone arrangement techniques. 'Ama no Hashidate' is located in the Tango area, the northernmost part of Kyoto Prefecture, known for the marvelous view of a long stretch of sandbar covered with green pines and white sands. Tango is also the birthplace of Tsuneko Kyogoku (Joshoin), wife of Prince Toshihito.

作庭に当たっては、最初に、約7万㎡の敷地に、近くの桂川から水を引き、舟遊びのできる池をつくり、池を掘った土を盛って高低差をつけ、山や谷をつくりました。この池泉の東寄り、松琴亭の前に広がる一郭には、石橋や石組の優れた技法により、日本三景の一つである丹後の"天橋立"の縮景が広がります。智仁親王の妃、京極常子＝常照院は丹後の出身でもありました。

'Ama no Hashidate' (Bridge of Heaven)
天橋立

'Wabi' and 'Sabi' 「わび」と「さび」

As visitors walk over the stepping stones along the garden path, collected from all over the country, they will find subtly placed ornamental stones, delicately arranged greenery, and effectively placed tea houses, waiting shelters and other ornamental structures. Katsura's landscape, an exquisitely designed nature-modeling, reveals 'wabi' (beauty in simplicity and austerity) and 'sabi' (beauty in something withered, lonely or tranquil).

苑路には各地から集められた飛石が敷かれ、庭には景石が置かれ、植栽によって仕切られ、茶亭や腰掛などの添景物が設けられています。自然を巧みに取り入れながら目立たぬところに技巧をつくし、「わび」と「さび」を表現しています。

Stone arrangement illustrating rough seashore
海岸の岩場（荒磯様）を表わす石組

Stepping stones along the garden path
苑路の敷石

'Oribe'-style stone lantern and ornamental stone
織部灯籠と景石

Embedded stone lantern and ornamental stone
生け込灯籠と景石

Chapter 2 Katsura Imperial Villa / 桂離宮   55

Influence of Western culture in garden techniques 西洋文化の手法

Katsura Imperial Villa was built during the Edo period, but the techniques used in the design show the influence of Western culture.

桂離宮は江戸時代に造られたものですが、作庭には多くの西洋文化と重なる手法が見られます。

✻ Perspective 遠近法

Visitors will notice 'depth' of distance, deeper than the actual conditions, when they stand at such points as 'Momiji no Baba' (Horse riding ground in acer trees) and 'Miyuki michi' (Noble path). The effects are the results of the perspective method, a technique to narrow the width of the features (like long garden path) toward the end to make viewers feel distance.

紅葉の馬場や御幸道などは実際よりも奥行きが感じられます。これは、直線の長い通路を先細りにして距離感を演出する遠近法が用いられているからです。

Miyuki michi (Noble path) appears longer than the actual distance
奥行きが感じられる御幸道

Maintained over 400 years   400年間にわたる維持管理

Visitors will be impressed by the allure produced by the integration of the greens in the garden and simple yet elegant buildings, approximately 400 years after the initial construction. This is exactly the outcome of the efforts by many workers at the Katsura Imperial Villa over a long period of time. Visitors should think about the importance of maintenance work in Japanese gardens.

築造から 400 年あまりを経ても、庭の緑と簡素な建物が織りなす美しさは、宮家を継ぐ人がなくなった後、1883 年から、代わりに維持管理に携わってきた元・宮内省や現・宮内庁の方々の努力の賜物です。この維持管理の重要性にも目を向けましょう。

Japanese garden maintained over 400 years
400 年維持管理されてきた庭

Chapter 2 Katsura Imperial Villa / 桂離宮   57

Layout of the garden and key facilities 庭の配置図

Suggested Route map 鑑賞のルート

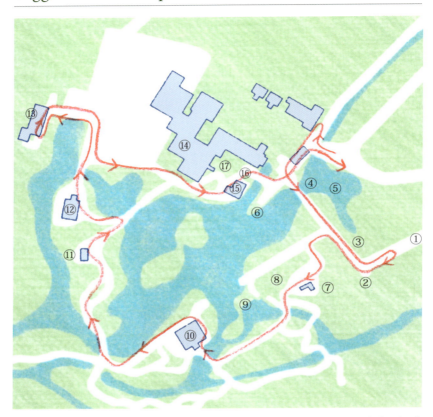

① Omote-mon (Main gate) ② Miyuki-mon (Gate for nobility) ③ Miyuki-michi (Noble path) ④ Dobashi (earthen bridge) ⑤ Boat hut ⑥ Sumiyoshi no matsu at Kikko misaki (Sumiyoshi pine kikko peninsala) ⑦ Soto Koshikake (outer waiting shelter) ⑧ Sotetsu yama (Cycas hill) ⑨ Suhama (Pebble beach) and Ama no Hashidate (Bridge in Heaven) ⑩ Shokin-tei ⑪ Shoka-tei ⑫ Onrin-do ⑬ Shoi-ken ⑭ Shoin (study halls) ⑮ Geppa-ro ⑯ Chu-mon (Middle gate) ⑰ Front garden of Okoshi-yose（Main entrance)

① 表門　② 御幸門　③ 御幸道　④ 土橋　⑤ 御舟小屋　⑥ 亀甲岬の住吉の松　⑦ 外腰掛　⑧ 蘇鉄山　⑨ 州浜と天橋立　⑩ 松琴亭　⑪ 賞花亭　⑫ 園林堂　⑬ 笑意軒　⑭ 書院群　⑮ 月波楼　⑯ 中門　⑰ 御輿寄前庭

Fence of Katsura Imperial Villa　桂離宮の垣根

* Katsura-gaki (Katsura fence) 桂垣

　The east side of Katsura Imperial Villa is bordered by a long span of bamboo fence (Sasa gaki), named after the Villa, 'Katsura gaki'. 'Katsura gaki' is famous for its unique design. Inside the fence is a forest of 'Henon bamboo', and live bamboo is leaned against the fence, bent downward at the top, and small branches tied to the fence. Thus, fresh green leaves always cover the fence.

　桂離宮の東側は『桂垣（笹垣）』と呼ばれる垣根に囲まれています。桂垣の内側は竹（ハチク）林です。この竹を垣根に向けて折り曲げ、竹の小枝の一部を垣根に編み込んで結び、青々とした竹の葉を覗かせます。

'Katsura-gaki' seen from inside (right) and outside (left)
内（写真右）と外（左）から見た桂垣

＊The inside of the fence is not included in the garden tour.
＊垣根の内側は見学ルートに含まれません。

* Ho-gaki 穂垣

　Ho-gaki is another bamboo fence with a different style, stretching from Omote-mon (Main gate) to 'Kuro-gomon' (Black gate). Hogaki uses the ear tips of bamboo, piled up horizontally and held between split bamboo pillars from the front and back. The top of the bamboo pillars is shaped like a spear, and intervals of pillars are set around 33 centimeters.

　穂垣は表門をはさみ外の道路から黒御門まで続く垣根です。横にした竹の穂を密に着せて、先を剣造りに尖らせた割竹を約33㎝の間隔で並べたつくりになっています。

Ho-gaki
穂垣

Chapter 2　Katsura Imperial Villa / 桂離宮　59

Stroll in the Garden   庭を巡る

Miyuki-mon, Miyuki-michi, Dobashi   御幸門、御幸道、土橋

The path from Miyuki-mon (Gate for nobility) to Koshoin (Old study halls) is called Miyuki michi (Path for nobility). The pavement style of Miyuki michi is called 'Arare koboshi (scattered hail)', embedding small stones with a slightly raised center of the path for better drainage. The vista method is adopted to this narrow path. Toward the end of Miyuki michi, Dobashi (earthen bridge) is located.

　御幸門から古書院に続く道を御幸道といいます。御幸道は小石を敷き詰めた道で、中央をやや高くし、水はけをよくしています。御幸道の細長い通路にはビスタの手法が見られ、御幸道の先に土橋があります。

Miyuki-mon
御幸門 ▼

▼ Miyuki-mon: a 'Munakado' style gate, made of logs of cork oak ('Abe maki') with barks unstripped, thatched roof, and gate door with vertical slits of split bamboo bars.
▼ 御幸門：アベマキの皮付きの丸太を用いた門柱、茅葺きの屋根、割竹（わりたけ）を縦に張った門扉から成る棟門（むなかど）形式の門。

Looking over Miyuki michi (Path for nobility)
御幸道をのぞむ

Earthen bridge
土橋

Chapter 2 Katsura Imperial Villa / 桂離宮   61

Sumiyoshi Pine tree hiding the view of a pond 池泉の眺めを隠す住吉の松

Passing over the earthen bridge, visitors find a pine tree down on their left side, named 'Sumiyoshi no matsu' (Pine of Sumiyoshi). The tree blocks the view of the pond (and the strolling-style garden). Seen from the opposite side of the pond, this pine tree catches the eye.

土橋を渡った先で、視線を左に移せば、「住吉の松」が目に入ります。この松は、先に広がる回遊式池泉庭園の目隠しになっています▼。一方、池泉の側から見た場合は、松は池泉のアイポイントになります。

Sumiyoshi no matsu
住吉の松

▼ In garden design, hiding a view of something (a pond, for example) by trees or walls stimulate expectations of visitors for the hidden items which are not visible. Such 'tricks' add pleasures to strolling in the garden.
▼ 造園では、樹木や塀などで池の景色を隠すことによって、隠された眺めに対する期待を高める働きが生じ、回遊を楽しいものとするといわれる。

Boating pond, boat hut (Ofunegoya) 舟遊びを楽しんだ池泉と御舟小屋

Water of the Katsura River is drawn into the Villa, a pond was excavated, and docks were built in the pond. A boat hut was also built, and the nobles are said to have enjoyed boating in the pond as well as in the Katsura River. Girders of earthen or wooden bridges connecting three islands in the pond were set high enough, so that boats can pass through.

桂川の水が引き込まれた池泉の各所には舟着場がつくられ、貴族たちは苑内を巡るだけでなく、苑内から桂川に出て、舟遊びを楽しんだといわれます。3つの島をつなぐ土橋や板橋には航行を考えて高い橋げたが設けられ、緩やかな反りがつけられています。

Simple boating hut with roofing. Boats were gathered here
御船小屋。屋根だけを葺いた簡素な小屋で、舟遊び用の舟が集められた

Momiji no baba, Soto Koshikake 紅葉の馬場、外腰掛

As visitors walk down Miyuki michi, toward the middle of the path, there is a small branch to the left which leads to another path called 'Momiji no baba' (Acer riding ground). In autumn, acer trees in the area turn breath-taking red. Visitors will find partial views of the pond and a tea house called 'Shokin-tei' through trees in the Ground.

Follow a narrow lane to the left from Momiji no baba, visitors will be brought to 'Soto koshikake' (outer waiting shelter). A small toilet called 'Kazari (or Suna) secchin' is installed beside the shelter. Suna (which means 'sand') secchin is NOT for actual use, but is made for decorative purposes. Natural stones are placed and sand is piled. Across the Suna secchin, double-square-shaped water basin is placed, with a baseless stone lantern installed next to it.

御幸道を、土橋に行きつく手前で左に曲がると、秋にはモミジが美しい「紅葉の馬場」と呼ばれる道に入ります。木々の間からは池が見られ、歩を進めると松琴亭の対岸に出ます。また、この紅葉の馬場から枝分かれした小道を左に進むと、その先に外腰掛が見えてきます。外腰掛の横には飾り雪隠といわれる装飾用の砂雪隠があり、自然石が置かれ砂が盛られています。砂雪隠の斜め前には二重枡形の手水鉢が置かれ、横には生込み灯籠が設けられています。

Momiji no baba
紅葉の馬場

Waiting shelter, stepping stones
外腰掛とその前の飛石

Cycas hill preparing for winter 蘇鉄山の冬支度

In front of the outer waiting shelter, visitors will face 'Sotetsu yama' (Cycas hill), a scene more familiar in tropical regions. These Cycas trees are said to be the gifts from the Shimazu family of southern 'Satsuma' domain, one of the most powerful feudal lords during the Edo period. Cycas trees were popular in the Edo period. At some shrines and temples, Cycas trees are often seen. The photo below right is Cycas trees, ready for winter.

外腰掛からは南国を思わせる蘇鉄の植栽が見えます。これが蘇鉄山です。蘇鉄は薩摩の島津家から献上されたものといわれます。江戸初期には人気のあった植木で、神社仏閣には今でもしばしば蘇鉄が見られます。右下の写真は、冬支度をしたソテツです。

Sound of waterfall

Visitors will notice the sound of a waterfall, if they strain their ears, as they walk past the waiting shelter.The sounds come from a small waterfall, named 'Tsuzumi no taki' (Waterfall of hand drum). The height of the waterfall is approximately 30 centimeters. Using two pieces of flat stone, the waterfall is carefully designed to echo sounds of water around.

〈ふっと耳を澄ますと鼓の滝の音が〉

御腰掛を過ぎるころ、耳を澄ますと滝の流れ落ちる音が聞こえてきます。これは「鼓（つづみ）の滝」という落差 30cmほどの滝です。大小 2枚の平石を組み合わせて水を落とし、水音があたりに響くようにつくられています。

'Tsuzumi no taki' 鼓の滝

Chapter 2 Katsura Imperial Villa / 桂離宮　65

Stone beach, Pond as 'Ama no Hashidate'   洲浜と天橋立を模した池泉

As visitors leave the shelter behind and walk down the garden path, a landscape of a pond and stone beach will suddenly welcome them. Across the water stands the tea house Shokin-tei. A stone arrangement with a large piece in the center, a stone beach and a small 'Misaki'-style stone lantern, a stone arrangement with a pine tree to resemble an 'island', stone bridges stretching across such 'islands' together illllustrate a famous landscape 'Ama no Hashidate' (Bridge in Heaven).

In this composition, the pond symbolizes an 'ocean', the stone beach paved by flat round stones sticking into the pond as a 'cape', with a 'Misaki'-style stone lantern sitting on a pedestal placed at the tip of the beach.

苑路を進むと、突然視界が開け、洲浜のある池泉の風景が広がります。松琴亭を対岸から眺めた景観です。大きな立石を中心にした石組、洲浜とその先にある岬灯籠、松を植えて小島と見立てた石組、小島を渡り継ぐ石橋など、天橋立をイメージした景観です。

大海を表す池泉には、平らな丸い石を敷きつめた洲浜が突き出し、その先端に中台より上を用いた岬灯籠を据えて岬と見立て、海の風景を描きます。

Stone beach viewed from garden path
苑路から見た洲浜

Calm surface of the pond reflecting 'Ama no Hashidate'
池泉に映える〝天橋立〟

Chapter 2 Katsura Imperial Villa / 桂離宮   67

Shokin-tei overlooking 'Ama no Hashidate' 天橋立を望む松琴亭

　Visitors walk across the Shirakawa bridge, placed in front of Shokin-tei tea house. Looking back at the end of the bridge, a view of 'Ama no Hashidate' and Misaki-style stone lantern placed at the tip of the stone-paved cape is so beautiful.

　Shokin-tei has thatched Irimoya (hip-and-gable) roof and walls are daubed with Osaka clay. Inside the crawling entrance of the tea house is matted with 'Sanjo daime', a special set of Tatami (straw mat) for the tea ceremony, and there are eight windows equipped with paper screens to take in light. In the first room, a hearth of one-tatami-mat size is equipped toward the pond side for cooking and heating purposes and guests will enjoy views of changing seasons in the garden over the windows on three sides. The paper sliding door is patterned with blue and white checks, which has a rather contemporary feel despite the fact that it was created some 400 years ago.

　On the west side of Shokin-tei, a dock made by cut stone is built. Stepping stones to go up and down the bank and a baseless stone lantern are installed.

Blue and white checkered pattern of paper sliding door
市松模様のふすま

　松琴亭の入口にある白川橋を渡って振り返ると、天橋立と洲浜の岬灯籠の眺めが広がります。
　松琴亭は茅葺入母屋づくり、壁は大坂土の茶室で、躙り口の内側は茶室用の畳である三畳台目が敷かれ、八窓の囲いになっています。一の間の池泉寄りには一畳ほどの石炉（調理と暖房を行う）が設けられ、三方の窓からは四季の変化を眺めることができます。室内の青と白の市松模様のふすまは、400年近く前のものにしてはモダンなデザインといわれます。この松琴亭の西側には切石の船着き場があり、ここには土手を上り下りする踏み石や生込み灯籠が見られます。

Shokin-tei and mirror lake seen from opposite side of pond
対岸から望む松琴亭と水鏡

View of the pond and Shokin-tei
松琴亭と池泉の風景

Shoka-tei looking down the pond 池泉を見下ろす賞花亭(しょうかてい)

An arch-shaped earthen bridge spanning over a stream of the pond leads guests to a gloomy trail which climbs around a small hill of cedars. At the end of the trail stands Shoka-tei, another tea house standing at the peak of 'Nakashima' islet. Shoka-tei is built at the highest elevation in the whole property, although the height is only five to six meters from ground level. Azalea in early summer and bush clover in autumn bloom around the tea house, and guests can enjoy good views of study halls and 'Atago yama' (Mt. Atago) through trees.

池泉にかかるアーチ状の橋を渡り、スギの木立により日中でも薄暗い道を回るように登ると、賞花亭が姿を見せます。これは中島(なかしま)に建つ茶室です。盛り土によるもので、わずか5、6mの高低差ですが、園内では一番高い場所にあります。初夏にはツツジ、秋にはハギが咲き、木々の間に新御殿や愛宕山を見ることができます。

Shoka-tei
賞花亭

Bridge whose girder and other elements are designed to let boats pass underneath
舟が航行できるように橋げたの高さなどを計算した橋

Shoka-tei surrounded by Japanese cedar trees
スギの木立に囲まれた賞花亭

Onrin-do (Mortuary tablet hall for the Hachijo family)   宮家の位牌を祀る園林堂

As visitors leave Shoka-tei behind, Onrin-do will come into their sight on the left, a three-room mortuary tablet hall for Hachijo family. At one time, all tablets of the family, including Prince Toshihito's, were placed in the hall.

Under the eaves, a stretch of lane paved by small stones surrounds the hall. Raindrops fall into the lane, instead of directly hitting earthen ground, so mud and clay will not be produced. A pair of stone lanterns is placed adjacent to Onrin-do. Next to the stone lantern, a hand wash basin is installed ahead of stepping stones.

賞花亭を下ると、左手に見えるのが園林堂です。仏を安置した三間の御堂です。かつて智仁親王の本尊をはじめ宮家代々の位牌が祀られていました。軒下には小石を詰めた雨落ち敷きが設けられ、土の跳ね返りを防いでいます。園林堂の脇には一対の石灯籠があります。灯籠の脇には、飛石の先に手水鉢が見られます。

Onrin-do sitting ahead of earthen bridge
土橋から見る瓦葺の園林堂

Stone lantern beside Onrin-do
園林堂の脇にある灯籠

Stepping stones and hand wash basin
飛石と手水鉢

Triangular-shaped stone lantern, modern design

A triangular stone lantern is placed on the right of the path on the way from Onrin-do to Shoi-ken. Sitting at the foot of a hedge, the lantern is easily missed. All parts of the lantern are triangular: 'kasa' (umbrella), 'hibukuro' (fire space), 'chudai' (middle base), and 'ashi' (foot).

〈現代的デザインの三角灯籠〉

園林堂から次の茶屋、笑意軒へ向かう途中に、三角灯籠があります。生け垣の足元にあり、見逃しやすいので注意しましょう。笠も火袋も中台も足もすべてが三角形です。

Chapter 2 Katsura Imperial Villa / 桂離宮

Shoi-ken, unique for its round windows 丸い窓が特徴の笑意軒

Shoi-ken is a tea house, standing in front of a rectangular part of the pond. Shoi-ken is known for its six unique round windows, all different in size and lattice-work design. A large piece of sharply cut gold leaf diagonally spreads over a wall covered by checkered velvet beneath a wide window. The unusual design is said to be a 'product of chance' during some repair work.

On the north side of Shoi-ken lies the pond, and two lines of stone stairs are built to approach the water, where a boat dock made of cut stones lies. A low stone lantern, called 'Sanko' (Three lights)-style, sits in the grass near the dock. The short lantern is made of only umbrella and fire space, and windows of the fire space are shaped like a sun, moon and star.

大きさや格子模様が異なる土壁を塗り残した６つの下地丸窓が独特な笑意軒は、四角い池に面した茶室です。窓下の市松模様のビロードの壁は、金箔が鋭く切り込む意匠で知られています。記録によれば補修によって偶然生まれたデザインとされます。

手前には池が広がり、二筋の石段を岸辺に下りると切り石でできた舟着き場へと通じ、その草むらには、笠と日・月・星を表す窓をもつ火袋を重ねた、背の低い三光灯籠が置かれています。

'Sanko' (Three lights, or Sun-Moon-Star) stone lantern in the grass near the dock
草むらにある三光灯籠

Shoi-ken seen from across the pond
対岸から見た笑意軒

'Nobedan' (stone-paved pathway) in front of Shoi-ken

Stone-paved pathway in front of Shoi-ken is called 'Sō (Informal style) no nobedan', which is made of natural stones only. Other than informal 'Sō', there are 'Gyō'-style (Semi formal) which uses both natural and cut stones, and 'Shin'-style (formal) which uses only cut stones. ('Shin', 'Gyō', 'Sō' of stone-paved path)

〈笑意軒の前の延段〉

笑意軒の前の延段は「草（そう）の延段」と呼ばれます。大小の自然石を集めた延段です。延段には、自然石と切り石を使った「行（ぎょう）の延段」、切り石だけを使った「真（しん）の延段」があり、これらを合わせて「延段の真・行・草」といいます。

'Sō'-style stone-paved pathway
草の延段

Chapter 2 Katsura Imperial Villa / 桂離宮   75

Shoin (Study halls) lined up like flying geese　雁行形に並ぶ書院群

　　As guests follow the path from Shoi-ken through 'Ume no baba' (Horse riding ground in plum trees) to an open space (said to be a ground for ancient football 'kemari'), a series of 'Shoin' (Study halls) shows up: 'Koshoin' (Old study hall), 'Chushoin' (Middle study hall), 'Gakki no ma' (Music instrument hall), and 'Shin Goten' (New palace). Each building was constructed at a different time, on a diagonal line like f lying geese. Koshoin and Chushoin are said to be ideal spots to admire the harvest moon in autumn. The Moon viewing veranda of Koshoin is stretched toward the pond for a good view of the Moon overnight.

　　笑意軒から土橋の手前の道を曲がり、かつて梅の馬場と呼ばれた苑路を抜けて蹴鞠の広場に出ると、書院群が姿を現します。古書院、中書院、楽器の間、新御殿から成り、雁が並んで飛ぶ姿のように斜めに配置される建て方を雁行形といいます。古書院と中書院は、中秋の名月を愛でるに適した場所とされ、古書院の池に向かって突き出した月見台からは、一晩中、月を楽しめます。

Stepping stones in front of Shoin buildings
書院前の飛び石

Gentle slopes surrounding Shoin buildings are covered with moss
書院周りのなだらかな苔の斜面

Moon viewing veranda of Koshoin
月見台

Chapter 2 Katsura Imperial Villa / 桂離宮   77

Geppa-ro, the tea house for watching the moon 月を愛でる月波楼(げつぱろう)

Behind the Shoin halls stands Geppa-ro, a tea house to enjoy moon viewing. The pond at the foot of Geppa-ro will become a mirror to reflect a beautiful image all night. During a tea ceremony on the veranda, guests will enjoy the view of Shokin-tei across the pond. In autumn, beautifully colored leaves can be seen from the north window.

書院群の先に、月を愛でるための茶室、月波楼があります。眼下の池が水鏡(みずかがみ)となり、月の影が一晩中映し出されます。縁側で茶の湯を楽しみ、池越しに松琴亭を眺め、秋には北の窓から、紅葉を楽しむことができます。

Geppa-ro is a tea house open to the outside.
Fresh air flows in across an earthen floor
外気が土間から流れ込む開放的な御茶屋

The view of the pond at the foot of Geppa-ro
月波楼から見る池の眺め

Looking out Shokin-tei
松琴亭を眺める

'Chu-mon', Lindera umbellata fence　黒文字の垣根、中門

　As visitors walk down stone stairs of 'Geppa-ro' and proceed to 'Chu-mon' (middle gate), a small tea garden shows up behind them, where a hand wash basin, cut stone-paved path, and a handful of stepping stones are displayed. From Chu-mon, a fence made of branches of 'Kuromoji' (*Lindera umbellata*), known for its pleasant scent, stretches along a garden path down to the Noble path.

　月波楼から石段を下りて中門へと進む途中、露地正面に手水鉢が目に映り、切り石の延段や飛石なども見えます。中門から御幸道までの苑路に沿って香しい黒文字垣が続きます。

Chu-mon
中門

Nobedan, stepping stones in the front garden seen through Chu-mon
中門から見える前庭の延段、飛石

About stepping stones

In Katsura Imperial Villa, quite a few stepping stones are used. A unique feature of these stones is that they are produced in diversified regions, not just Kyoto, but from Hyogo, Tokushima, Kagawa and other places. Differences in colors, shapes, sizes and placement in the garden produce myriad appearances for these stones.

〈飛石について〉
桂離宮には多くの飛石があります。その特徴は石の産出場所が違うことです。石は京都のほか兵庫や徳島、香川からも運ばれてきました。地域により異なる自然石の色、形、大きさ、そして庭に据える位置により表情は異なります。

Chapter 2　Katsura Imperial Villa / 桂離宮

Okoshi yose (Main entrance of Study halls)　書院群の玄関、御輿寄

Okoshi yose is the main entrance to the Study halls. In the center of Okoshi yose, a huge piece of granite stone is placed. The size is so huge that it is said that a line of six people can take off shoes along the stone, the reason it is called 'Six-pair shoe removal stone'.

The compositions of the building of Okoshi yose, moss-covered front garden, and stepping stones are based on the golden ratio. The stone-paved path made by cut stones is called 'Shin no Tobi-ishi' ('Shin'-style steping stone).

御輿寄は書院群の玄関であり、大きな御影石が置かれています。この上で6人が横一列に並んで沓を脱ぐことができることから、「六つの沓脱」と呼ばれます。

桂離宮の御輿寄の建造物とその苔むした前庭、飛石の比は黄金比率で構成されており、この切石を使った石組は「真の飛石」と呼ばれています。

'Shin'-style stone-paved path in front of main entrance
御輿寄前の飛石

Visitor information 利用案内

Web site ホームページ
http://sankan.kunaicho.go.jp/english/guide/katsura.html

Location 場所
Katsura Misono, Nishikyo-ku, Kyoto-city 615-8014
Tel. (+81-75)-211-1215

〒615-8014 京都市西京区桂御園
電話　075-211-1215

Transportation 交通
Get off at Kyoto station (Shinkansen)
By Hankyu Railway Kyoto Line: get off at Katsura station and walk about 20 minutes.
By Kyoto City Bus: get off at Katsura Rikyu mae station and walk about 8 minutes.

新幹線京都駅下車
〔京都市内から〕阪急電鉄京都線で桂下車、徒歩約20分。または市バスで桂離宮前下車徒歩約8分。

Closing days 参観休止日
Closed on Mondays (if Monday is national holiday, next Tuesday will be the closing day), during December 28 to January 4, and special event days.

参観休止日は、月曜日（月曜日が国民の祝日となるときは、翌火曜日）、年末年始（12月28日〜1月4日）、行事等の実施で支障のある日。

Tour schedule (only guided tour is available) 参観開始時間
Tours leave at 9, 10, 11am, 1:30, 2:30, 3:30pm. (Each tour accepts up to 35 persons, and takes about 1 hour)

午前9時、10時、11時、午後1時30分、2時30分、3時30分（定員は各回35名、所要時間約1時間）

Fence and earthen wall
垣根と土塀

CHAPTER 3

THREE GARDEN ELEMENTS AND ORNAMENTAL ITEMS
of the Japanese garden

日本庭園 — 三要素と添景物

Stone bridge lies between Kanzan-tei and Shinzan-so
観山亭と神山荘を結ぶ石橋

Japanese gardens often use a technique called "shakkei", meaning borrowed scenery, which incorporates landscapes from nature such as distant mountains or rivers into their own composition. The design consists of three elements, e.g. water, stone and plants, to reproduce natural scenery in a miniature form. In Chapter 3, different types and roles of three garden elements and ornamental items are described, introducing examples taken from Shinsen-kyo garden of the Hakone Museum of Art.

日本の庭園は、自然の風景を借景として取り入れ、
水と石と樹木から自然を模し、凝縮してつくられる庭です。
ここでは、箱根美術館の神仙郷を中心に、庭を構成する池泉、
石、植栽の三要素と添景物を取り上げ、その種類と役割を紹介します。

Pond: Core of the garden 庭の中心となる池泉

Japanese gardens evolved with pond 池泉を中心に発達した日本庭園

A pond in a Japanese gardens originates from a small puddle or stream built on the south side of a house, taking water from a nearby river, in an aim to abate Japan's hot and humid summer. In Jodo (Pure Land) style gardens, lotus is planted in ponds.

Since ancient times, a variety of items came to be placed in lotus ponds: islets, Mt. Penglai, Mt. Sumeru, and islands named 'crane' or 'tortoise' as symbols of longevity. Also, styles/formats of stone arrangement and functions/positions assigned to special stones (yaku-ishi) were developed. Further, numerous items of geographical features like capes, inlets, 'Ariso'▼ seashores and cobble beaches were built as parts of gardens, which stood for local picturesque scenes.

Thus, ponds and streams, originally created to provide cool air in a garden, turned out to be scenes to cherish, and became key features of Japanese 'Shuyu'-style gardens▼ built for entertainment such as boating on the pond or poetry writing by the streams.

池泉は、日本の蒸し暑い夏の気候に対処するため、近くの川から水を引き、建造物の南側に池や流れをつくりだしたことに始まります。古くは、池は神が宿る場と考えて、池泉に蓮を植えました(蓮池)。やがてこの蓮池に、日本の象徴である島を置き、神が下りる中島にはあの世を託す蓬莱山、須弥山、長寿を願う鶴亀島などが設けられ、池の配石や流れの役石が考えられました。さらに、地方の景勝地を模して岬や入江、荒磯▼や洲浜などもつくられました。

こうして池や遣水は、涼を求めると同時に愛でる対象になり、舟遊式庭園▼のように舟遊びを楽しみながら詩歌を吟じる遊興の中心になったのです。

▼ 'Ariso': Seashore with rough waves.
▼ 荒磯：波が激しく打ち寄せる磯。

▼ 'Shuyu'-style garden: a garden with a pond for boating and writing poems.
▼ 舟遊式庭園：池泉に舟を浮かべて詩歌を楽しむ庭。

Stone placement in a stream in moss garden
苔庭の流れの配石

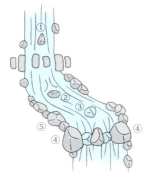

Stone arrangement in a river or a stream
川や流れの配石

① Water-dividing stone　水切石
② Water-surpassing stone　水越石
③ Base stone　底石
④ Width-reducing stone　横石
⑤ Bank-holding stone　つめ石

Chapter 3 Three garden elements / 庭園の三要素　85

Garden waterfall 水の景を表わす庭滝(にわたき)

　The height of a waterfall in a Japanese garden is, in general, 2 to 3 meters. How water falls down and the sounds of water echoing in the waterfall basin are adjusted by stone arrangement. A dry waterfall does not use actual water, and visitors imagine how water should flow through the stone placement. Dry waterfalls could be better understood with knowledge about spirits of 'wabi' (beauty of simplicity and austerity) and 'sabi' (to see beauty in something withered). In Japan, water in a garden falls down in a form like waterfall, while in Europe, water in a garden spouts up into the air like a fountain.

　庭滝の高さはわずか2〜3mです。配石(石の置き方)によって水の落とし方や滝つぼに響く水音を調整し、さまざまな種類が生まれました。水を使わず、配石を見て水が流れるさまを想像する枯滝もあり、枯滝にはわび・さびの精神が求められます。
　また、日本では水を滝として上から落とすのに対して、ヨーロッパでは噴水として下から噴き上げます。水の景の表現方法には大きな違いが見られます。

Ryuzu waterfall in a pond beside Nikko-den
日光殿横の池泉の龍頭(かれたき)の滝

Names of stones in a garden waterfall
庭滝に使う滝石・役石の名称

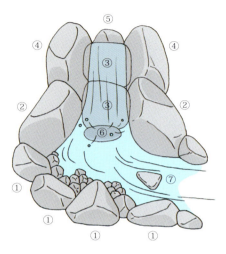

① Bank stone 護岸石
② Base stone 根石
③ Mizuochi-ishi 水落石
　(Stone set near the base of the fall)
④ Takizoe-ishi 滝添石
　(Stone placed near top of the waterfall)
⑤ Water-dividing stone 水分石
　(Stone placed outside of the basin of the fall)
⑥ Mizu-uke-ishi 水受石
　(Stone placed at the bottom of the fall)
⑦ Namiwake-ishi 波分石
　(Stone which changes direction of water flow)

Types of waterfall
滝の種類

Waterfall stone arrangement　滝石組

Dry waterfall　枯山水

Chapter 3 Three garden elements / 庭園の三要素　　87

Garden bridges: A landscape accent　景観の視点になる庭橋

A bridge in a garden is a symbolic ornamental item that indicates the style of the garden. Arched bridges and flat bridges will bring contrasting colors in a garden atmosphere and appearance. Simple earthen bridges using logs and stone bridges provide themes and accents in the landscape. A covered bridge (bridge with a roof) or a bridge with parapet can prevent sunlight, wind, rain or accidents.

橋は庭園様式を示す象徴的な添景物です。橋に反りをつけた反橋や反りのない平橋を組み合わせて庭に変化をつけます。丸太を並べただけの簡素な土橋や、石を組み合わせた石橋などは庭にテーマ性を打ちだし景観を引き締めます。橋に屋根をつけた廊橋や欄干をつけた呉橋は、日差しや風雨、事故を防ぐことができます。

Types of bridges
橋の種類

Flat bridge
平橋

Stone bridge passing over a stream
遣水を渡る石橋

Arched bridge with parapet
欄干をつけた反橋

Chapter 3 Three garden elements / 庭園の三要素   89

Stones: The base of garden structure 庭の骨格をつくる石

Stones as dwellings of God 神が宿る場としての石

In Japanese gardens, stone arrangement is a framework of the overall design, and it has been seen as dwellings of god. Stones used in the arrangement are collected from mountains, rivers or oceans. Stones from mountains have rough edges, while river stones are more often flat, with most corner edges gone. Ocean stones are even smaller. The composition and colors of stones are different, depending on where they are produced, and so is the selection of where a stone is placed. In small gardens, all the stones should be of the same origin.

日本庭園では、庭の骨格をつくり、神が宿る場として石組が作られてきました。石組には、山や川、海から採石した山石、川石、海石を用います。山石は角がごつごつした荒々しい石、川石は角が取れて平たくなった石、海石はさらに小さくなった石です。採石してきた場所によって石の性質や色、使用場所が異なります。小さな庭では産出場所が同じ石を使います。

Stone part names
石の部分名称

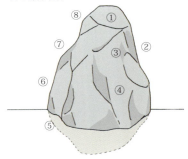

Stone garden in Sekiraku-en　石楽園の石の庭

① tenba (crown)　天端
② hana (nose)　鼻
③ ago (chin)　あご
④ mituki (front)　見付き
⑤ neire (root)　根入れ
⑥ mikomi (side)　見込み
⑦ syakuri (dent)　しゃくり
⑧ kata (shoulder)　肩

Placement of more than 2 stones 2つ以上の石を組み合わせる配石

'Ishigumi' (stone arrangement) means placement with more than two stones. The number of stones to be arranged should be odd such as 3, 5, 7, except for two, as odd numbers are considered good luck. A garden design made with these stone arrangements is called 'stone garden'.

Traditional stone arrangement places stones to form a scalene triangle, with kazari-ishi or ornamental stones at the center.

石組とは、2つ以上の庭石を組み合わせたものをいいます。用いる石の数は、二石組を除けば、三石組、五石組、七石組などの奇数です。奇数は縁起がよい数です。この石組によって庭の造形をつくり出したものを石庭といいます。石組は、飾石、または景石を中心に不等辺三角形を描くように据えるのが伝統的な手法です。

Stone arrangement and stone momentum
石組の種類と気勢（石の勢い）▼

Cover stone base with plants
石の脇の根締めによる処理

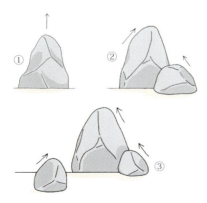

① Single stone 一石
② Two stone arrangement 二石組
③ Three stones arrangement 三石組

▼ Direction of momentum of stones seen in appearance (shown in arrows).
▼ 見たときに感じられる石の勢い（矢印の方向）。

Chapter 3 Three garden elements / 庭園の三要素   91

Pavement, stairs, masonry of stone　草・行・真による敷石・石段・石積み

Stone pavement is used at public squares and long garden paths. Stone stairs are made of stone pieces, and masonry is a roughly piled up stone wall used for earth retaining.

To make these structures, both natural and processed (cut) stones are used. Using only natural stones is a style called 'Sō', meaning informal, while combination of both stone types is a style called 'Gyō', which is semi-formal, and using only processed stones is 'Shin', a formal style.

敷石は広場や長い苑路に用いる石の舗装、石段は石を組み合わせた階段、石積みは土止めなどを行うときの荒削りな石垣をいいます。自然石のほか切石を用いることもあり、自然石だけを使用するものを「草」、自然石と切石を使用するものを「行」、切石だけを使用するものを「真」と区分しています。

Stone pavement
敷石

Above, Below: Masonry works
石積み（上・左下）

Stone stairs
石段

Chapter 3 Three garden elements / 庭園の三要素

Stepping stones: How to ensure walkability 足元を確かにする飛石

Stepping stones are believed to be the idea of tea master Sen Rikyu in the 16th century, when he built a hut for tea ceremonies in a remote, secluded place. The climate in Kyoto, in particular, is very humid, and garden soil will easily be covered by moss. It also rains a lot in Kyoto, impeding walkability for tea ceremony guests. At the tea ceremony, they often sprinkle water in the garden, which makes walking difficult. Stepping stones are a solution for these problems. Stepping stones should be more comfortable to walk on than on soil, weather-proof, and beautiful. Visitors proceed in the garden following the stepping stones.

飛石は16世紀、千利休が世俗から離れた奥深い地に茶室を設けたときに、茶庭に取り入れたといわれます。とくに京都は湿度の高い土地で苔が生えやすく、雨も多く足さばきが悪い上に、茶の湯ではしばしば打ち水をするので、さらに足元が悪くなります。この足元をカバーし、裾汚れを防ぐために飛石が必要とされました。石の上を歩くので足ざわりがよく、天気が悪くても歩みを妨げず、置かれた石の姿が美しいことが条件です。この飛石をたどって園内を巡ります。

Shoe-removing stone, stepping stones
沓脱石（くつぬぎいし）と飛石

'Chu-mon' (gate between outer and inner tea gardens) and stepping stones 中門と飛石

How to place stepping stones
飛石の打ち方

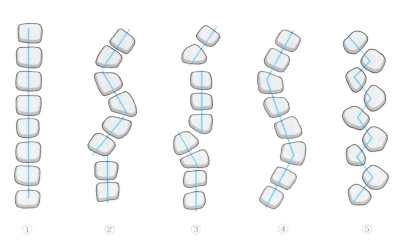

① Direct-strike 直打ち／② Two-row strike 二連打ち／③ Two-Three-row strike 二三連打ち
④ Wild geese path 雁打ち／⑤ Plover path 千鳥打ち

Chapter 3 Three garden elements / 庭園の三要素　　95

Nobedan (stone-paved rectangular path)   足の運びを促し、足元を飾る延段

'Nobedan' is a rectangular stone-paved path in the tea garden, with a width of 75 to 90 centimeters and length of 3 to 5 meters, generally set higher than ground level. Used in combination with stepping stones, nobedan offers tea ceremony guests better conditions to walk. Besides such practicality, nobedan holds decorative purpose, with three styles of 'Shin' (formal), 'Gyō' (semi-formal), and 'Sō' (informal).

延段とは、地表より高く、一定の幅（75〜90㎝）と長さ（3〜5m）をもつ敷石のことをいいます。飛石と組み合わせ、歩きやすくします。延段も真、行、草があり、庭を美しく飾ります。

Nobedan, stepping stone at Sho-tei (MOA Museum of Art)
樵亭前の延段と飛石（MOA 美術館）

Types of nobedan
延段の種類

Gyō style　行

Sō style　草

Shin style　真

Plants add seasonal tastes 四季の風情を際立たせる植栽

Plant to form scalene triangles 不等辺三角形に植えて庭に動きを出す

In Japanese gardens, pine has been integral, because of its evergreen leaves. Greenery should form a scalene triangle. In a formal style, pine comes at the center position, 'shin', while 'tai' (competing plant, but not excelling pine) or 'soe' (set-off plant) positions should be chosen from coniferous trees such as *Cryptomeria japonica* or *Chamaecyparis obtusa*, evergreen trees like *Ternstroemia gymnanthera*, *Ilex integra*, *Castanopsis* ssp., *Quercus myrsinifolia*, or deciduous trees like *Ginkgo biloba*, *Prunus mume*, *Acer* ssp., *Zelkova serrata*, *Prunus* ssp. (Japanese Sakura). Bamboo or bamboo grass are used for undergrowth, the bottom of the fence, or sleeve fence. In the tea garden, humble flowers such as camellia, azalea or quince are planted.

日本の庭の主役は秋でも冬でも緑が美しいマツです。植樹は不等辺三角形が基本で、正式には、マツを「真」として、「対」や「添え」には、スギ、ヒノキなどの針葉樹やモッコク、モチ、スダジイ、シラカシなどの常緑樹、イチョウ、ウメ、カエデ、ケヤキ、サクラなどの雑木と呼ばれる落葉樹が植栽されました。さらに、下草や塀・垣根や袖垣に、タケやササなどが用いられます。茶庭では、ひっそりと咲くツバキ、ツツジ、ボケなどが茶花として庭を飾ります。

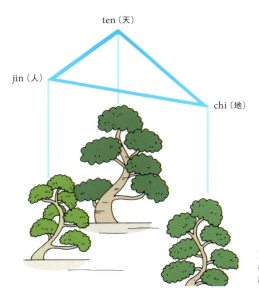

Planting trees based on the Yin-Yang and the Five Elements theory
庭木の配植：陰陽五行説に基づく配植

Beautiful landscape composed of smaller and larger Pine trees
松の大小で景をつくり出す

Bamboo should be planted in odd numbers
竹庭：竹は奇数本植える

Chapter 3 Three garden elements / 庭園の三要素　　99

Specimen tree 庭に生気を生み出す役木

Planting trees in front of (or behind) focal points in a garden, such as a gate, fence, sleeve fence, lantern, wash basin or by the pond/lake brings about liveliness to the garden. Liveliness is a concept like a fresh air that passes through the garden. Such functions and utilities of trees are called 'yakuboku', or Specimen trees.

門扉や垣根、袖垣などの外構や灯籠、手水鉢などの添景物、池のそばなど苑内の要所に木を一本植えると、庭に生気が生まれます。生気とは邪気に対する正しい気という意味で、今風にいえば庭を通り抜けるすがすがしい空気と考えればいいでしょう。この木の役割と効用を役木といいます。役木にはいろいろな種類があります。

Specimen tree in front of lantern
灯障(ひざわ)りの木

Types of specimen trees
役木の種類

Hanging over a gate　門冠りの木

Behind a stone lantern　灯籠控えの木

Trees planted at fence-end for accent　垣留めの木

Hanging above wash basin　鉢請けの木

Concealing a Lantern　灯障りの木

Hanging above a pond　池添えの木

Chapter 3　Three garden elements / 庭園の三要素　　101

Cold protection, support posts 草木を守る支柱と防寒

In regions with cold climates, there are a number of methods to protect trees and greenery from cold weather. Frost protection, 'yuki tsuri' (supporting branches by ropes hanging from top of a tree to prevent branches from breaking by the weight of drifted snow), and snow fences are commonly used. Also, to protect tree trunks from cold air and strong afternoon sun, wrapping them with straw mats or hemp cloth is often done. Placing straw at the tree base is an effective way to keep trees warm. Support posts, in a couple of styles, are attached to avoid trees from falling down, and they are also used to hold large branches or trunks which are extending in horizontal directions ('hozue'). A trellis can be used for creeping plants.

寒い地方では植栽を守るために、霜を防ぐ霜よけ、重い雪から木や花を守る雪吊りや雪囲いを使い、それ以外にも木肌を寒さや強い西日から守るために幹にこもや麻布を巻く幹巻き、根元には敷き藁などを敷くこともあります。また、庭木が倒れるのを防ぐために支柱（八つ掛け・鳥居掛け）を立てたり、枝や幹が横に伸びている場合に丸太をＴの字に組む方杖によって枝を支えたり、ツルをのばす植物には藤棚のように棚を設けて花の美しさを引き出す方法もあります。

Cold protections
防寒の方法

Yuki tsuri 雪吊り

Frost protection 霜除け

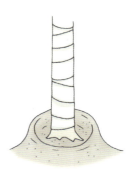

Mikimaki 幹巻き

Different designs of posts
支柱の種類

Hozue post 方杖

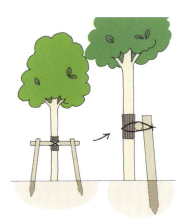

Torii post 鳥居掛け

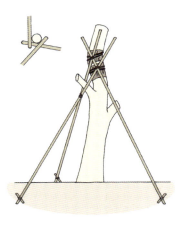

Yatsugake post 八つ掛け

Chapter 3 Three garden elements / 庭園の三要素   103

Ornamental items 庭の風景を引き締める添景物

Stone lanterns cast light on feet 足元を照らす石灯籠

Stone lanterns were initially made as memorial towers set in temples. In the 16th century (late Muromachi period) to Azuchi Momoyama period, when tea gardens evolved as a style, stone lanterns were placed in them, intended to light at the feet of guests. In the course of the flourishing of tea ceremony culture, stone lanterns also developed varieties.

Stone lanterns are placed at or around: Corners of a garden path, crossroads, the entrance to the tea room, a hand wash basin, gate, waiting shelter, or toilet. Near the pond in a garden, lanterns are put at the cape or cobble beach. They are also set near gazebos or shrubbery.

もとは寺の供養塔だった石灯籠は、16世紀の室町時代末期から安土桃山時代にかけて発展した茶庭では露地に置かれ、茶会に招かれた客人の足元を照らす灯りとして利用されるようになりました。以降、石灯籠の種類も増えていきます。これらは、茶庭では園路の曲がり角、分かれ道、茶室入口、蹲踞・門・腰掛・雪隠付近などに置かれ、水辺では岬や洲浜に、あるいは四阿などの建造物や植え込みなどに設置されています。

Yunoki-style lantern at Shinwa-tei
真和亭にある柚木型灯籠

104

Stone tower　庭に奥行きや広さを見せる石塔（層塔）

Stone towers are seen in gardens constructed during the Edo period. For example, placing a five-story stone tower among trees and plants intends to make visitors imagine a five-story pagoda (a larger structure than the tower), and have them feel the garden has more depth. Or visitors may think the stone hills are larger than reality, compared with the stone tower. On top of the stone tower, a pagoda finial is attached. Tiers of tower roofs are in odd numbers, seen as good luck, ranging from 3 to 13.

石塔は植栽の中に、たとえば五層塔を設けて、実物の五重塔を想定させて奥行きを出したり、石塔との比較から岩山などを大きく見せたりする効果があります。塔の上には相輪(そうりん)が突き出し、塔の屋根は縁起のよい3〜13重の奇数層になっています。

A garden with stone tower
石塔のある庭

Various types of stone lanterns seen in Katsura Imperial Villa

Stone lanterns originated as votive offerings to temples and shrines, for family prosperity or safety on a long journey. Later, stone lanterns came to be used in tea gardens as lighting for the garden paths or ornamental items to decorate landscape in the garden.

〈桂離宮にみる石灯籠〉

灯籠は一家の繁栄や道中・海上の安全などを願って神仏に献上したのが始まりです。茶庭が登場して以来、苑路の照明に、庭の景観を引き立てるために使用されるようになりました。

Above left: Manshuin-style lantern　上左：曼殊院型灯籠
Above right: Firefly-style lantern　上右：水蛍灯籠
Below: Snow-viewing lantern　下：雪見灯籠

Fences, Sleeve fence　目隠しや仕切り直しに用いる庭垣や袖垣

Fences are set for various purposes: Demarcation, guiding, concealment, alteration of landscape and others. Materials are, in most cases, very common such as bamboo, ears, branches and brushwood, all available in the tea garden.

庭垣は、園内の区切りや誘導、目隠し、風景の仕切り直し（修景）などの目的のために設けられます。材料は、たとえば茶庭では、多くの場合、竹や穂、枝、柴など庭内にある身近な材料が使われます。

＊Yotsume-gaki　四つ目垣

The basic structure of 'yotsume-gaki' (four-eyed fence): Between main and intermediary posts, cut bamboo is layed across at different heights and tied at crossing points to vertical bamboo slats, which stand at intervals, with cords. Occasionally, horizontal bars and/or vertical slats are further covered by cut bamboo.

四つ目垣の基本構造は、親柱と間柱の間に、何段か胴縁をかけ渡し、立子を立てて、立子と胴縁の交点を結束します。必要に応じて立子と胴縁を挟み込んで押縁としたり、立子の天端に玉縁を取りつけることもあります。

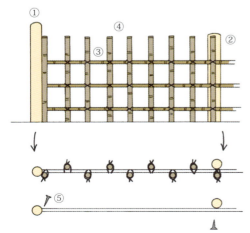

① Oyabasira (main post)　親柱
② Mabashira (intermediary post)　間柱
③ Dobuchi (horizontal bar)　胴縁
④ Tateko (vertical slat)　立子
⑤ Hammering a nail into a Dobuchi　胴縁にくぎを打つ

Types of fence
垣根の種類

Yotsume-gaki (Four-eyed fence)
四つ目垣

Ho-gaki (Bamboo ear fence)
穂垣

A sleeve fence▼ is usually a small fence stretching out from the edge of a house or tea room. Bamboo, wooden boards or brushwood are used as materials, in order to partially block garden view, alter a landscape in the garden, or to partition. This 'Koetsuji gaki' is used as a sleeve fence, a relatively minor use for 'Koetsuji'.

袖垣▼は、建物の一部から袖のようにのぞく小さな垣根をいいます。竹や板、柴を用いて目隠しにしたり、庭の景色の転換を図ったり、仕切りにするのが目的です。この光悦寺垣は、一般的な用途である仕切り垣ではなく、袖垣として使われています。

Sleeve fence of Fujimi-tei　富士見亭の袖垣

▼ At the foot of a sleeve fence, a stone ('sashi-ishi') is placed to block moisture rising from the soil, and trees are planted at fence-end for accent ('kakidome').
▼袖垣の足元には地面からの湿気を押さえるための差石（さしいし）が置かれ、垣留（かきどめ）の木が添えられる。

Types of fences
垣根の種類

Koetsuji-gaki
光悦寺垣

Chasen-gaki (Tea whisk fence)
茶筅垣(ちゃせんがき)

Mino-gaki(straw raincoat fence)　蓑垣(みのがき)

Teppo-gaki (Musket fence)
鉄砲垣

Chapter 3 Three garden elements / 庭園の三要素

'Tsukubai' and 'Chozubachi'　身を清める蹲踞と手水鉢

'Tsukubai' (low wash basin), consisting of a 'Chozubachi' (hand wash basin) and trump stones, originated from stone setting to surround a fountain and keep the water clean. In the beginning, hand wash basin was only placed under the eaves or in the earth floor, or beside a veranda. The present style of combining wash basin and trump stones is said to be developed after the basin was introduced into tea garden. Before entering tea room, guests of tea ceremony stoop at tsukubai, wash their hands and rinse their mouth.

蹲踞は、湧き出る泉を清潔に保つために石で囲んだのが始まりで、手水鉢とその役石から構成されます。もとは手水鉢だけで、軒下や土間、縁先などにあったものが茶庭に取り入れられて、蹲踞という形になったといわれます。茶室に入る前に、蹲踞で身を低くして手を清め、口を漱ぎます。

Hand wash basin　手水鉢

Structure of 'tsukubai'
蹲踞の構造

Horizontal plan
平面図

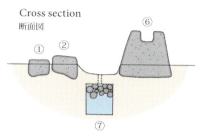

Cross section
断面図

① stepping stone　飛石
② front stone　前石
③ 'sea'　海
④ hand lamp stone　手燭石
⑤ warm water-pail stone　湯桶石
⑥ hand wash basin　手水鉢
⑦ water drainage system　排水

Perspective
パース

Placement of hand wash basin

In 'tsukubai' (Stone setting with hand wash basin), hand wash basins made of natural stone are to be placed outside of 'umi' (sea), while those made of processed stone in square or round shapes can be set either in or outside of 'umi'.

〈手水鉢の配置〉

蹲踞は手水鉢が自然石の場合は〝海〟の外に置くが、加工した方形や円形の手水鉢は〝海〟の中に置いてもかまいません。写真は加工した手水鉢による蹲踞。

Chapter 3　Three garden elements / 庭園の三要素　111

'Suikin-kutsu', 'Kakei', 'Shishi-odoshi' 音を楽しむ水琴窟・筧・鹿おどし

To enjoy water sound in a garden, Suikin-kutsu (Water harp), Kakei (Bamboo conduit), Shishi odoshi (Deer scarer) are used. A water harp often uses drain water from tsukubai. A big jar is buried upside down beneath the 'umi' (sea) drain system of tsukubai, and echoes the sound of water droplets, resembling a harp.

A bamboo conduit is a pipe to send water to tsukubai. In a deer scarer, water from conduit pours into cut-end of bamboo pipe, until that end becomes heavier than the other closed end. But once water-filled side goes down, the load will instantly be released, sending the closed side back until it hits a stone and makes a clack sound.

庭に水を引いて、水の音を楽しむ方法として、水琴窟、筧、鹿おどしなどがあります。水琴窟は、蹲踞で手を洗い、口を漱いで水を流したときに、その水が落ちるのを利用してつくられることが多く、排水口の下に甕を逆さにしたような共鳴装置があり、水が落ちるたびによい音を響かせます。

筧は水源から引いた水を送る竹筒です。水路を曲げるときは駒頭を用います。筧から手水鉢に水を落とす技術にはいろいろあります。

鹿おどしは、筧からたまった水が落ちると、元に戻るときに石にあたって音を出し、筒の中で音を高めて「コン」と、鳴り響く仕掛けになっています。

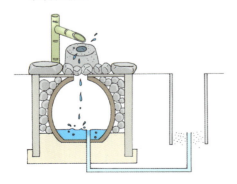

Structure of water harp
水琴窟の構造

Suikin-kutsu 水琴窟

Kakei
筧

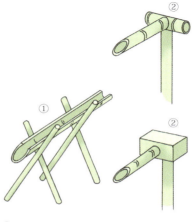

① Kakei 筧
② Komagasira (change of the flow of water) 駒頭

Shishi-odoshi
鹿おどし

Chapter 3 Three garden elements / 庭園の三要素 113

Tea room, Tea house　一期一会を楽しむ茶室・茶亭

Tea garden, Chatei and Chashitsu　茶庭・茶亭・茶室

In a divided tea garden, waiting shelters are set up in an outer tea garden, which is from the entrance to Chu-mon (middle gate), as well as in an inner garden, from Chu-mon to tea room. The waiting shelter is set for tea ceremony guests to wait for their host to come and call the guests. The structure is very simple, with single roof, a bench covered with tatami (straw mat) or wood board or slatted board. Tobacco tray, and charcoal heaters in winter, are also placed for guests.

　茶庭は、露地口から中門までの外露地、中門から茶室までの内露地に分かれ、それぞれ腰掛が設けられています。腰掛は茶室・茶亭に入るまでの客人の待ち合わせの場です。片屋根などの簡素な建物で、畳や板、すのこが敷かれ、煙草盆や冬は火鉢なども置かれます。

Inner garden　内露地

Waiting shelter, Stepping stones　腰掛と飛石

Entrance of Chatei　茶亭の入り口

Crawl-in entrance of Chashitsu　茶室の躙り口

A tea room which guests enter directly via an earth floor is called Chatei, while those which guests enter via nijiri guchi (crawl-in entrance) is called Chashitsu. Stepping stones, sword racks and refuse hole are set near the entrances.

When holding a tea ceremony, the alcove is decorated with a hanging scroll and flowers. A tea kettle to make hot water and folding screen for portable brazier will also be placed in the tea room.

茶室のうち、土間から直接上がるものを茶亭、躙り口から出入りするものを茶室といいます。茶亭や茶室の入口にも、飛石や沓脱石、刀掛け、塵穴などが見られます。

茶会を催すときには茶室に茶掛け、茶花などで床の間を飾り、茶釜や風炉先屏風などを整えます。

Folding screen for portable brazier and tea kettle
風炉先屏風と茶事の湯を沸かす茶釜

'Mizuya', a space for preparations of tea ceremony
茶事の準備と片づけをする水屋

Hanging scroll and flowers decorate the alcove in a tea room
床の間を飾る茶掛けと茶花

Chapter 3 Three garden elements / 庭園の三要素　115

Steps to enjoy light green tea   薄茶の飲み方

① Host makes light tea, and serves to a guest, with the front of tea bowl facing the guest.
② Guest will say to the next guest, "Excuse me for going ahead of you."
③ Guest will express gratitude to host, bowing politely.
④ Pick up tea bowl with the right hand, put it on the left hand, hold it up reverently.
⑤ Rotate tea bowl twice to the right by right hand, drink tea from an edge other than the front.
⑥ Drink up the tea in three and a half sips.
⑦ Once finished, wipe bowl edge with index finger and thumb.
⑧ Wipe the fingers with paper
⑨ Rotate tea bowl twice to the left, and put it back to the initial position (depending on the school)
⑩ Look at tea bowl with low glance, take in the hand and look closely, and view the whole again with both hands placed on floor.
⑪ Return tea bowl, with front side facing the host.

① 亭主は薄茶を立て、茶わんの正面が客人に向くようにひざ前に出す。
② 客人は隣の客人に「お先に」とあいさつする。
③ 亭主には「お点前頂戴いたします」とていねいにお辞儀をする。
④ 茶わんを右手で持って左手に乗せ、感謝の気持ちを込めて押し頂く。
⑤ その茶碗を右手で手前（右側）に2回まわして正面を避けて味わう。
⑥ お茶は三回半に分けて飲む。
⑦ 飲み終わったら、吸い口を人差し指と親指の先で拭う。
⑧ 汚れた指を懐紙で拭う。
⑨ 今度はむこう（左側）に2回まわし、畳の縁の外側（裏千家）または内側（表千家・武者小路千家）の元の位置に戻す。
⑩ 最後に低い姿勢で茶碗を眺め、手に取ってつくりを拝見して置き、最後に両手をついてもう一度全体を眺める。
⑪ 亭主に正面が向くように茶碗を返す。

Where to place tea bowl during the tea ceremony may differ by school
流派によって、茶わんの置き場所など異なることがある

Chapter 3 Three garden elements / 庭園の三要素   117

Profile

Saki Kosugi

President of Kosugi Zohen Co. Ltd. in Tokyo, Japan
Born in 1946 as a grandson of family of gardeners whose origin traces back more than 300 years, Mr. Kosugi devoted over 40 years to building Japanese gardens, landscape designing and landscape construction. Based on his abundant experiences, Mr. Kosugi also designed and built a lot of rooftop gardens and wall greenery. His gardening expertise, which combines Japanese traditional gardening methods and modern tastes, draws acclaim outside Japan as well: Mr. Kosugi already constructed Japanese gardens in South Korea, Azerbaijan and Bahrain. He occasionally travels abroad to deliver small lectures on the history and techniques of Japanese gardening.
In 2009, Mr. Kosugi was granted the Medal of Honour with Yellow Ribbon by the Emperor for his industriousness.

Ryuichi Kosugi

Managing Director of Kosugi Zohen Co., Ltd.
Born in 1951. Graduated from School of Economics, Meiji University. Joined Kosugi Zohen in 1973. Certified skilled worker of landscape gardening (Grade 1). Acknowledged in 2009 as 'Excellent Master of Construction Works' by the Ministry of Land, Infrastructure, Transport and Tourism. Certified in 2010 as Registered fundamental skilled worker in landscape gardening. Certified in 2014 as 'Production Master' by the Ministry of Health, Labour and Welfare. Plenty of experiences as leader of garden construction projects in overseas sites, including Azerbaijan, Bahrain and Georgia.

Fumiharu Kosugi

Senior Vice President of Kosugi Zohen Co., Ltd. since 2012. Born in 1971 in Tokyo. Worked for an advertising agency after graduating from College of Economics of Rikkyo University. Joined Kosugi Zohen in 2006, working as next top of Kosugi Zohen. Working to introduce Japanese garden culture to overseas.

Andreas Hamacher

Dr. Andreas Hamacher Director International Business Division
Born in 1961 in Frankfurt am Main, Germany. Obtained Master's Degree in Landscape Architecture from Hannover University/Germany and PhD degree in Landscape Architecture (research on ancient Japanese Gardens) from Chiba University/Japan. At Kosugi Zohen Co., Ltd. he conducts seminars for foreigners on how to construct and maintain Japanese Gardens. As director and project manager at Kosugi Zohen Co.Ltd. he is in charge of all Japanese Gardens constructed outside Japan.

著者プロフィール

小杉左岐 こすぎさき

小杉造園株式会社代表取締役

1946年、東京・世田谷で300年以上続く家柄の植木屋の3代目として生まれる。日本庭園だけではなく、マンションの環境緑化デザイン・施工にも40年以上かかわる。そのノウハウを生かして屋上・壁面緑化など外部環境のデザイン・施工も多く手掛ける。伝統的技法と現代のセンスを生かした庭造りの実績は海外でも評価が高く、これまでに韓国、アゼルバイジャン、バーレーンで日本庭園の施工と管理を行っている。また、招かれて日本庭園の歴史や技術の発信もしている。平成21(2009)年黄綬褒章受章。

小杉龍一 こすぎりゅういち

小杉造園株式会社専務取締役

1951年、東京・世田谷生まれ。明治大学経済学部卒業後、1973年小杉造園株式会社入社。1984年より現職。1級造園技能士。2009年優秀施工者（建設マスター）表彰（国土交通省）、2010年登録造園基幹技能者。2014年ものづくりマイスター（厚生労働省）。アゼルバイジャン、バーレーン、ジョージアなど海外工事の現場指揮多数。

小杉文晴 こすぎふみはる

小杉造園株式会社常務取締役

1971年東京都生まれ。立教大学経済学部卒業後、広告代理店に勤務。2006年小杉造園株式会社に入社し、4代目修行中。海外へ日本庭園を発信。2012年より現職。

Andreas Hamacher ハマハ アンドレアス

小杉造園株式会社海外事業部部長代理

1961年ドイツのフランクフルト生まれ。ドイツのハノバー大学卒業、工学修士。国費留学生として千葉大学園芸学部庭園デザイン学研究室に留学、庭園学で学術博士取得。千葉大学では2年間、園芸専門学校では8年間の教授実務経験。小杉造園では毎年外国人のための日本庭園施工・メンテセミナーを企画・実施。海外では日本庭園作庭プロジェクトを企画・実施、プロジェクトマネジャーとして活躍。

Japanese Garden and Garden Culture to the World
世界に日本の庭文化を

Corporate Profile

　Kosugi Zohen Co., Ltd., founded in 1943, is a landscaping company in Setagaya, Tokyo, Japan. Founded as a farm in 1673 (the Enpoh era) in Shimo-Kitazawa village in Ebara county, Musashi Province (currently Kitazawa in Setagaya, Tokyo), Kosugi's business later extended to nursery of trees during the Taisho period. Kosugi flourished in gardening business in the Showa period.
　Condominiums and apartment houses gained popularity as a style of housing in Japan around 1964 when Tokyo Olympic Games were held, and Kosugi Zohen has shifted emphasis of business more to maintenance of trees planted on the premises of such housings, reflecting the changes in housing market environment.
　Thanks to its long corporate history, Kosugi Zohen now can offer a wide array of services which include consultation, design, construction and maintenance of trees and gardens for our customers.
　Kosugi Zohen's high level of garden techniques made it possible to successfully transplant extraordinary-sized trees, including a 300-year old pine tree and a 500-year old Gingko tree. Kosugi Zohen has also won a gold medal in the 39th WorldSkills competition.
　Kosugi Zohen is the only member company from Asia of the European Landscape Contractors Association (ELCA). Kosugi Zohen also offers Japanese culture and garden seminars with hands-on curriculum every year at its training center in Atami, Shizuoka Prefecture, for landscape architects and students from all over the world. Saki Kosugi contributes to cultural exchanges through activities like small lectures on Japanese culture outside Japan.

Kosugi Zohen won a gold medal at the 39th WorldSkills Competition
第39回技能五輪国際大会で金メダルを獲得

Kosugi Zohen successfully transplanted a 300-year old Japanese red pine tree
樹齢300年のアカマツの大木の移植

沿革

　1943（昭和18）年の創業以前は、1673年（延宝年間）より武蔵国荏原郡下北沢村（現在の東京都世田谷区北沢）にて農業を営む。大正時代より植木生産も行い、昭和初期からは植木職として発展。
　1964年の東京オリンピックのころから日本では集合住宅（マンション）が一般化し始め、小杉造園においては、日本での住環境の変化を素早く感じ取り、個人邸から集合住宅の植栽管理へとかじを切る。
　小杉造園はその歩みの中で、お客様の庭園のコンサルティングを始め、デザイン、施工、管理と幅広い対応能力を身につけてきている。また、樹齢300年の赤松や樹齢500年のイチョウの移植など多くの樹木の移植にも成功し、技術力においても高い評価を得ている。
第39回技能五輪国際大会では金メダルを獲得し、世界一の名誉にも浴する。
　アジア企業では唯一ELCA（ヨーロッパ造園建設業協会）の加盟が許され、毎年、世界各国から研修生を招き、自社の熱海研修所での日本文化や庭園の研修、世界各地での講演など幅広い活動と国際貢献を行っている。

A Japanese garden constructed by foreign students during a Kosugi's garden seminar
日本庭園セミナーでの海外学生の作品

Students from Europe who participated in a Japanese garden seminar
セミナーに参加したヨーロッパ諸国の学生

Awards

2016　City of Setagaya Award for Advanced Enterpriser in gender equality
2014　Grand prize (Governor of Metropolitan Tokyo award) in human resource training program by medium/small enterprises
2013　Best prize in 'Shinkin Dream Weaver' award, offered by the Metropolitan Tokyo Shinkin Banks Association
2011　Second place in the 9th 'Courageous Management' Award by the Tokyo Chamber of Commerce and Industry
2010　Grand Prix: Tokyo International flower & garden show 2010
2007　Gold Medal: 39th WorldSkills Competition (Shizuoka, Japan)
2006　Governor's prize: Hibiya Park Gardening Show 2006
2004　1st place: Hibiya Park Gardening Show 2004
2004　2nd place: International Roses and Gardening Show 2004

受賞歴（抜粋）

平成28(2016)年：平成28年度世田谷区男女共同参画先進事業者賞受賞
平成26(2014)年：平成26年度東京都中小企業人材育成大賞知事賞受賞
平成25(2013)年：東京都信用金庫協会　最優秀賞しんきんゆめづくり大賞
平成23(2011)年：東京商工会議所「勇気ある経営大賞」優秀賞
平成22(2010)年：東京インターナショナルフラワー＆ガーデンショー
　　　　　　　　　2010 ベスト・オブ・ザ・ショーガーデン
平成19(2007)年：第39回技能五輪国際大会造園部門金賞
平成18(2006)年：第4回日比谷公園ガーデニングショー
　　　　　　　　　ベランダガーデン部門東京都知事賞
平成16(2004)年：第2回日比谷公園ガーデニングショー
　　　　　　　　　ガーデン部門金賞、ベランダガーデン部門金賞
平成16(2004)年：第6回国際バラとガーデニングショウ
　　　　　　　　　コンテスト・ベランダガーデニング部門準優秀賞

Japanese garden built in Heydar Aliyev Park, Baku, Azerbaijan (October 2015)
アゼルバイジャンの首都バクーの大統領公園に完成した日本庭園（2015年10月）

Bahrain Japan Friendship Garden opened in Bahrain (February 2015)

バーレーンで作庭した「バーレーン日本友好庭園」（2015年2月）

Japanese garden built in a botanical garden, Tbilisi, Georgia (October 2016)

ジョージアの首都トビリシの植物園に完成した日本庭園（2016年10月）

Friendship garden opened in Okku Park (Siheung-Si, Gyeonggi-do, Korea October 2010)

韓国 京畿道始興市（キョンギ道シフン市）オック公園に作庭した「友情の庭」（2010年10月）

※ Torii gate is built in the garden as a symbol of Japan.
※ 鳥居は日本のシンボルとして建てている。

Address

KOSUGI Kosugi Zohen Co., Ltd.
Kitazawa 1-7-5, Setagaya-ku, Tokyo, Japan 155-0031
Tel. +81-3-3467-0525
Fax. +81-3-3467-0970
http://www.kosugi-zohen.co.jp/

KOSUGI 小杉造園株式会社
〒155-0031 東京都世田谷区北沢1-7-5
電話 03(3467)0525
FAX 03(3467)0970
http://www.kosugi-zohen.co.jp/

参考資料

『桂離宮　ポケットガイド3』宮内庁京都事務所監修（財団法人菊葉文化協会）
『桂離宮　日本建築の美しさの秘密』斉藤英俊著（草思社）
『桂離宮と東照宮　日本美術全集16　江戸の建築1・彫刻』大河直躬編纂（講談社）
『古寺巡礼112　よくわかる　日本庭園の見方』齋藤忠一監修（JTBキャンブックス）
『すぐわかる日本庭園の見かた』尼崎博正監修（東京美術）
『茶庭・小庭づくり　施工プランと実例21』淡交社編集局編（淡交社）
『日本庭園の伝統施設　鑑賞と技法の基礎知識』河原武敏著（東京農大出版会）
『日本庭園のみかた』宮元健次著（学芸出版社）
『歴史と文化を楽しむ　日本庭園鑑賞のポイント55』宮元健次著（メイツ出版）
『庭園植栽用語辞典』吉河功監修／日本庭園研究会編（井上書院）
『造園大辞典』上原敬二編（加島書店）

箱根美術館、桂離宮に学ぶ美の源流

日本庭園

2017年1月21日　初版第1刷発行　　2025年6月30日　初版第4刷発行

著　者：小杉左岐・小杉龍一・小杉文晴・ハマハ　アンドレアス
発行者：藤本敏雄
発行所：有限会社万来舎
　　　　〒102-0072
　　　　東京都千代田区飯田橋2-1-4 九段セントラルビル803
　　　　電話　03(5212)4455
　　　　E-Mail letters@banraisha.co.jp

デザイン／引田 大 (H.D.O.)
イラスト／遠野 桜
写真協力／箱根美術館・小杉造園・小杉左岐
編集・執筆協力／戸田真澄・株式会社オフィス宮崎

印刷所：株式会社エーヴィスシステムズ
© Saki Kosugi, Ryuichi Kosugi, Fumiharu Kosugi, Andreas Hamacher 2016 Printed in Japan

落丁・乱丁本がございましたら、お手数ですが小社宛にお送りください。
送料小社負担にてお取り替えいたします。
本書の全部または一部を無断複写（コピー）することは、著作権法上の例外を除き、禁じられています。
ISBN978-4-908493-04-1

Published by Banraisha Co., Ltd.
Kudan Central Bldg. 803, Iidabashi 2-1-4, Chiyoda-ku, Tokyo, Japan 102-0072
http://www.banraisha.co.jp/
E-Mail : letters @ banraisha.co.jp

Japanese Gardens : Learning the Origins of Beauty from Hakone Museum of Art and Katsura
Imperial Villa
Copyright © 2017 by Saki Kosugi and Ryuichi Kosugi and Fumiharu Kosugi and Andreas Hamacher
English translation copyright © 2017 by Kosugi Zohen Co., Ltd.
All rights reserved. Printed in Japan.